Call Me Mistress

Call Me Mistress
Memoirs of a Phone Sex Performer

Karen Ainslee

Cover Design
Nancy Terzian Design
Sausalito, California

Cover illustration by Sage Callaway
San Anselmo, California

Published by Karen Ainslee
Portland, Oregon

ISBN 978-0-9637672-0-2
Library of Congress Catalog Card Number 93-79544

PREFACE

This book is about my personal experiences as a phone sex "fantasy performer." I am not a therapist and have no special training in understanding sexuality or treating sexual dysfunction. My observations, therefore, are not professional opinions or diagnoses. They are simply my perceptions. I offer them for entertainment and for information. These are real experiences, and I believe that they have something significant to say about human sexuality as it is expressed in fantasy.

My field of observation is limited by a self-selection process. I have no way of knowing whether my callers represent the general population; I suspect that they do not.

The majority of my callers are white middle-class heterosexual or transvestite men. I do not know to what degree my observations hold true for minorities, heterosexual women, gay men or lesbians. I suspect that the dynamics of fantasy are not much different for these other groups, although perhaps some of the specifics are. Obviously, many of the racial and ethnic stereotypes would be different or non-existent for minority callers.

I decided to get into doing phone sex because I believed I would be good at it and enjoy it. I am and I do. I understand the dynamics of fantasy, I am sensitive and nonjudgmental enough to tune in to the callers and respond to their needs, and I am a skillful actress. I do some of the best fake orgasms in the business.

Although I enjoy doing live phone sex, I would not be interested in doing recorded phone sex. The magic of live phone sex lies in the interaction between two people. In live phone sex, the customer can get his own unique needs met. Recorded phone sex, on the other hand, is canned, standardized. Even if the customer can select which type of call he would like, he has no way of controlling timing or intensity.

It is also easier to control access to live phone sex. It can be kept away from minors. Personally, I feel strongly against involving children in any form of pornography or prostitution.

It may be argued, of course, that the availability of any kind of pornography may encourage acting-out behaviors, which could be directed against children. I feel confident, however, that there are sufficient controls on the phone sex activities in which I am involved, to prevent their use against children.

I believe, in fact, that this type of phone sex is safe from all of the forms of exploitation to which most other pornography is prone. I feel comfortable doing this work. I don't feel exploited. And although I may be exploiting my customers, they are choosing to be exploited, and I am not responsible for that choice.

Because phone sex has been so intense and intriguing for me, I have felt a tremendous need to share my experiences and insights. When I started talking to my friends about phone sex, several of them kept saying, "You should write a book." Well, here it is.

CONTENTS

1

What It's All About

"Hello?"

"Hi, Jim! This is Ginger. How're you doin'?"

"I'm pretty good. How are you?"

"Oh, I'm fine. Would you like to know what I look like?"

"Sure, tell me."

"Well, I'm five foot five, about medium build, 130 pounds, and my hair is blonde, about shoulder length. My tits are 38-C, with big nipples..."

"Mmmm..."

"My waist is 25 and my hips are 38..."

"Sounds great!"

"I've got long sexy legs, and my pussy hair is blonde."

"You sound luscious! How old are you?"

"Twenty-five." (A blatant lie, but I sound younger than my true age, on the phone.) "So...how can I help you out tonight?"

"Well, you can help me get off."

"Anything particular you have in mind?"

"No, just some good fucking."

"You've come to the right place for that. Tell me, are you in bed now?"

"I sure am."

"Are you naked?"

"Uh-huh."

"Is your cock hard?"

"It's gettin' there."

"Maybe I could play with it, huh?"

"Sure! Go ahead!"

"Mmmm. Let me take that cock in my soft warm hand and squeeze it! Could I taste it?"

"Oh, yeah! Please do!"

(I make licking and sucking noises, as he moans.) "Ooh, your cock tastes so good! Would you like to feel up my tits, feel how soft and warm they are?"

"I sure would."
"Squeeze my nipples, get them hard! Ooh, that gets me so hot, when you squeeze my nipples!"
"Yeah, I like it when they get hard!"
"Would you like to suck on them?"
"Oh, I'd love to!"

Yes, this is a typical beginning to a typical "hot-and-sexy" call. Most nights about half my calls fall into this category. During my shift, though, I might do a bisexual call, a couple of strict dominants, and perhaps a sensuous dominant or a "kinky." If it's a high-energy night, I might get lucky and do a story fantasy or a cross dresser call.

While most of the "normal" calls focus on the kind of directly erotic talk I've demonstrated above, the "dominant" calls have a different tone—one of abuse and degradation:

"Your ass needs to be fucked by this 12-inch dildo I've got, doesn't it?"
"Yes, Mistress."
"I'm shoving it up your ass now. Hurts, doesn't it?"
(Caller moans.) "Yes, Mistress. You can do anything you want to me, Mistress."
"All my girlfriends are here watching me fuck you, laughing at you. We're all going to take turns spanking you."
"Oh, please, Mistress! Don't let them do that!"
"Shut up, you slut! Who do you think you are, talking back to your Mistress?!"
"I'm sorry, Mistress. I know I deserve to get spanked."

No matter what type of call it is, though, the length of the call, when I worked for a service, was almost always seven minutes. Exceptions were story fantasies, which are fun, and difficult callers, who are not. Story fantasies generally go for ten or twelve minutes; difficult callers use up all their time and may or may not get off.

Seven minutes may seem like a short time to fuck, but remember that you don't have to mess with the physical realities, like taking off clothes, changing positions, getting two bodies coordinated, etc. You can do a lot in seven minutes on the phone.

An experienced performer once told me that I should be able to get my callers off in three to five minutes, and I probably could, but I feel that the quality would suffer. Having spent years in service industries, where customer satisfaction is the most important product, I feel an obligation to do at least a decent job, if not a perfect one.

Now that I'm working independently, I have a different clientele who tend to do longer calls—15 to 25 minutes, sometimes even 30 or 45 minutes or even longer. I also don't get a high volume of calls—one or two a day is average. But the first couple of years I worked for a phone-sex service, I was generally pretty busy, doing eight to ten calls a night. I'd usually have a break of at least five or ten minutes between calls, which gave my voice a chance to recover if I'd had one of those customers who has demanded a lot of screaming or groaning. (The cardinal sin in phone sex is to cough or clear your throat. This is similar to the prohibition against farting in prostitution.) Sometimes I had to drink some water or even gargle, and there were occasions when even that didn't work. I learned some tricks of swallowing hard and frequently, or talking in a lower than normal voice, to keep myself from coughing on the phone. Of course it goes without saying that I can't work when I'm too hoarse or congested.

Occasionally, I might stay on the line and talk with the guy for a while after the call is "done"—i.e., after they guy has come. I've had some pleasant chats this way, but there are also times when I feel invaded. Some callers are curious about me: do I do this for a living, or do I have another job? am I married? if not, do I have a boyfriend? does he know I do this? I fudge the truth a bit; I figure it's none of his business.

After each call, if there's anything particularly notable about the caller, I write myself short notes or abbreviations next to his name in my

notebook: "good energy!," "jerk!," "weird," "animals," "XV" for transvestite (cross dresser), stars (one to five) for exceptionally sensuous
callers. When I worked for the service, I would tally up what I had
earned each night; at the end of the week, I would total up the week's
take.

Sometimes as I drift off to sleep I wonder how some of my acquain-
tances would react if they knew how I had just spent the last couple of
hours. When I do reveal it to someone new, it's usually quite a bomb-
shell. To most people, phone sex is a little off the deep end. To me, it's
all in a day's work.

HOW PHONE SEX IS PERFORMED

Phone sex is the perfect second job. I work at home, at whatever time
I want, for as long as I want. When I worked for the service, I would
call in to the office and tell them I wanted to "come on call." When I
wanted to quit for the night, I would call them back and tell them I
was "going off." Often, to save myself the toll charge for calling the
office, I'd just tell them which call I wanted to make my last for the
night.

The company screened the calls for me. The customer called the office, whose number he had found in a magazine ad, and gave them a
credit card number. They checked his credit and determined what
kind of call he wanted: "hot and sexy," "bisexual," "kinky," "strict
dominant," "sensuous dominant," "submissive" or "cross dresser." The
office then called me, gave me the customer's phone number, type of
call ordered, and a time limit of 10, 12, 15 or 20 minutes. I then called
the customer back, collect, using my phone name, Ginger. A repeat
customer could request me specifically by asking for me by my phone
name. I got paid a little extra for these calls. (Now that I have my
own service, I give a price break to my regulars.)

Sometimes the customer could call me direct. This was cheaper for
him, and gave me more protection because the calls were actually
patched through the office: he called an office line and the line was
forwarded to me. My number never showed up on his phone bill.

Although I occasionally had trouble with customers calling me at home directly, this happened much more rarely than I feared it might when I first learned about this arrangement. As with any other obscene call, the most effective strategy is just to hang up. I never had one call back a second time.

Occasionally, the call was not obscene. It might just be a customer confusing my number with the office line. He'd usually say something polite like, "Can I get a call now?" Once in a great while I'd get a question about whether "we" sell videos, sex toys or lingerie, but I would just tell the caller no and refer him to the office number if he was persistent.

These intrusions weren't really the customer's fault. They didn't know that we worked out of our homes, and they probably really thought they were calling a business number. Even though the real office number shows up on their phone bill as a direct call, many of them were not bright enough to figure out the difference between the office and me. Or more likely, by the time they got their phone bill they didn't even remember what steps they went through to make the call.

When I worked for the service, almost all of the calls I did were long distance. I got very few calls in the same area code I was in. I talked to people all over the United States and Canada.

I used to wonder what the phone company operators thought of all this. Not that I told them why I was calling, but I did make a lot of collect calls in a short time. And since I got to know the voices of some of the operators, they probably also got to know mine. They were always polite, however: "Thank you, Ginger, and thank you for using AT&T."

The customer paid the company for the call, by credit card, and also paid the long-distance carrier for the toll charges. I got a commission on each call. Working for myself, I get all the money from the call, minus a fee to the credit card processor. And of course I have to pay all my advertising expenses.

Although the specified category of a call gives me an approximate idea of what to expect, there is a great variety within each type of call—more variety within some types than within others.

Here's a brief description of the official types of calls, although I go into them in more detail in the chapters about calls and callers.

HOT AND SEXY

This is pretty self-explanatory. It's the standard call. Sometimes the customer will ask for a "nympho" or for some specific physical characteristic, such as "a tall blonde," "an older woman with big tits," or "a young white girl" (usually from a white man, by the way).

BISEXUAL

The customer wants to fantasize that I have another woman with me. He watches while I make it with her. There are some variations on the bisexual call, which I'll talk about in later chapters.

KINKY

This is a catch-all. Sometimes these are really bizarre calls, but more often than not, these callers just think that "kinky" means "uninhibited."

STRICT DOM

This is sado-masochism ("S/M") stuff. The customer wants to be my slave, wants me to abuse and humiliate him. These calls can sometimes be interesting.

SENSUOUS DOM

This customer wants me to dominate him, but in a sensuous rather than abusive way. Sometimes he wants to be tied up, but he generally doesn't want to be abused. These guys usually love to be teased. I think they're great fun.

SUBMISSIVE

This is the opposite of the strict dom call. I am the one being abused. We don't get many of these calls. I do about one every two years.

CROSS DRESSER

This is a customer who cross-dresses—likes to put on women's clothes (usually lingerie). Sometimes he dresses up while I watch and admire him ("You're so cute and sexy"), sometimes I order him to dress up. Often, but not always, this type of caller wants me to abuse him. He usually wants to fantasize that he's a woman or perhaps a little girl. These men refer to themselves as "sissy boys." They are a type of sexual orientation different from either straight or gay.

Although these are the call categories that my company uses, I have my own category definitions. I've found that most of the types listed above don't really describe anything significant about the call. More important, I feel, are the callers' energy levels and attitudes about sex and fantasy. These are the ingredients that determine how I handle the call and how I feel about it.

THE PHONE SEX OFFICE

I only went in to the phone sex office a couple of times. It was a dull place—nothing sexual about it. Three or four operators answered the phones in a room just large enough to accommodate four desks and a TV set. On either side of the TV, windows looked out on the street below, which was in an area of the city that a gay friend of mine once described as a "straight pick-up scene." I would add the adjective "yuppie" to this. It's fairly clean and crime-free, with a lot of delis, moderate- to high-priced restaurants and bars, lots of places you can get espresso coffee. On weekend nights well-dressed couples roam the streets, many of them inebriated. During the day the clothing and make-up shops are open. Either way, there's plenty of money changing hands.

The phone sex office was on the third floor of an old storefront building. The furniture was old, too, and the room unimaginatively decorated. Undecorated would be a better word. Hand-written lists of bank telephone numbers hung from the walls—numbers to call for credit checks. Binders of computer printouts lay on the desks—lists of bad credit card numbers. (One of my long-term projects was to get the place more computerized.) Once the operators put up a pin-up of a scantily clad man, but the manager (a straight man) took it down; he didn't like things that degraded men.

Most of the operators smoked, and the TV was invariably tuned to the typical bad American shows—sex, violence and inanity. If you hung around for a while, you'd catch bits of our half of the conversations:

"Hello, may I help you?" (The standard greeting; we don't say, "Suzie's phone sex line" or anything like that.)

"Do you have a MasterCard or Visa?" "No, we don't take American Express." "No, you can't use your son's credit card for phone sex!"

"It's $15.95 for a ten-minute call if you're willing to accept a collect call; $19.95 if you want an 800 number." "No, you can't talk to someone right now; we're a call-back service, sir." "I suggest you try a 900 number, then. Good-bye."

"And what kind of a lady would you like to talk to, sir—hot and sexy, bisexual or kinky?" "A black woman with big tits, dressed in a red lace negligee? We just happen to have such a woman working to-night. Her name's Vivian; she'll be calling you back collect."

In between calls, the operators joked, gossiped, complained about their husbands or boyfriends, made fun of the callers—the usual women's conversations. There was more action down in the street than there was in the office.

I was usually insulated from all of this. The last time I paid a visit to the office was to take in an oversized dildo that one of my regular customers had sent me (I had convinced him that I was as obsessed with large cocks as he was—a tribute to my acting ability). We gave it away as a door prize at the next Christmas party. We wanted to use it as a baseball bat at the company picnic ("Look what they've got at their company picnic, Honey! Let's go over there!"), but children attend that event.

So Why Does It Work?

Phone sex is about fantasy—pure fantasy, limited only by the imagination, emotions and talents of the caller and the performer. This is what makes phone sex so intriguing to me: the lack of limitations. You can get anything you want in phone sex, anything your heart desires. All it requires is the ability to fantasize.

I am fascinated by this lack of limitation and by what it can reveal about our world view, values and emotional needs. Fantasy, like dreams, takes us into the world of non-directed, "right-brain" thinking. And although fantasies appear to be more direct, conscious and easier to interpret than dreams, still they often take on a life of their own and meander down paths that surprise us. They hover on the borderline between the conscious and the unconscious.

It is not true, by the way, that only women conjure up elaborate story fantasies about sex. Many men are equally creative in this area. This was one of the first stereotypes I had to give up when I started doing phone sex.

Not everyone, however, can fantasize. Some people just can't. In fact, some callers don't really use phone sex as a vehicle for fantasy. A lot of them are people who just get off on graphic sexual talk. This isn't the same thing as fantasy, but it works for them.

When I was working for the service,, I also occasionally got callers who just couldn't respond to phone sex on any level. They were generally polite. Thanks, but it's just not working for them, they explain.

I don't know if people who can't fantasize are more fortunate or less fortunate than the rest of us. I can't imagine living without fantasy, but I sometimes think that life might be simpler without it. It can be a distraction from dealing with real problems, and can even become an obsession.

But whatever effect fantasy has on the fantasizer, for us in the phone sex business it pays. And for me, not only has it paid; it has also provided me with entertainment and education.

2

Why's a Nice Girl Like Me Doing This?

ABOUT ME

For over 30 years I was a computer programmer and systems analyst. I loved my work in the business community, and I loved doing phone sex on the side. Both jobs involved dealing with people—their problems, limitations, demands, and needs. Both required flexibility, creativity and an ability to be nonjudgmental.

I also did volunteer work as a telephone crisis counselor. A lot of what I learned on the crisis line, I have applied to phone sex as well. On the crisis line, I learned not to let my value judgments prevent me from listening actively and being empathic—a skill which I use in phone sex, also. In both types of calls, the caller is the one who determines where the call is going and how much they will get out of it. The listener or performer is a facilitator for that process. As we said on the crisis line, "It's the caller's call."

Although I'm now self-employed in several endeavors, many people I know in my work or social life don't know about my sex work. In fact, because I keep my sexuality under wraps so much, many of them probably could not even imagine my doing anything like this. And sometimes living this double life is crazy-making. Although to me these different roles I play fit together well, it's hard to find other people who understand this.

Yet my fantasy-performer role is an important part of who I am. I wouldn't trade these experiences for anything.

Sometimes, when I'm sitting in a business meeting or a social gathering, I get flashes of thoughts such as, "Do I really go home from this and do obscene phone calls with men?" "What would people here think if they knew what I did in my evenings?" "I wonder what these people's secret sexual fantasies are!"

I have to admit that the "secret life" quality of the job intrigues me. It's also something that makes me feel "special"—that I am privileged to touch a part of my callers which they don't let anyone else see.

HOW I GOT STARTED

I got into phone sex through my "daytime" job. In the office where I worked, one of my co-workers had a daughter who worked for the phone sex company as a dispatcher (not as a performer). I was intrigued; I had always wanted to try phone sex, but had hesitated because I thought I would have to audition and didn't know how well I could do under observation. But as I questioned my colleague about the work, she allayed my fears. There was no audition. If I wanted to try it, I could just start. If I wasn't suited to the work, I would soon find out for myself.

Still, I put off starting for several months, until I was laid off from my daytime job. Then I had the added incentive of economic necessity. That was enough to get me going, although I was still frightened the first few nights. I was exhilarated after my first successful call, though. After I hung up the phone, I jumped around the room shouting, "It worked! It worked!"

I've come a long way since that first call. I've been through a lot of feelings—frightened, overwhelmed, cynical, angry, powerful, compassionate, accepting. As with most of life's significant experiences, I started out with expectations and preconceptions and ended up with more questions than answers. This book is about my process as much as it is about my experiences.

BEING A FANTASY PERFORMER

A fantasy performer is part entertainer, part counselor (someone to listen and accept) and part companion (someone to assuage loneliness). The job requires good acting skills, good listening skills, sensitivity, creativity, flexibility, and the ability to talk graphically about sex. Being something of a ham doesn't hurt either—that's where the performer part comes in.

The most important quality for a phone sex performer to possess, though, is an open mind—a lack of judgmentalism. As I got more experience, I found that I was dropping more and more of my judgments. I talked to so many different people about so many bizarre things, and I had so many of my stereotypes shattered, that I simply had to give up judging. Judging would have shut me off from the most interesting calls, at least in the sense that I wouldn't have been able to carry the calls to the fulfillment that the callers needed.

Herein lies the key to being a successful performer: being able to "go with the call" wherever it leads. And that is not always predetermined at the beginning of the call. Like anything else that human beings do, fantasy has a life of its own, a life that takes off only when the limitations of judgment and inflexibility are removed.

There are, however, some limitations, some ground rules, to phone sex. There are some things that I will not tolerate from my customers, and there are some things which I feel are off limits to me. My rules for my customers are:

> Don't ask me personal questions. If you do, don't expect truthful answers. My personal life is none of your business.
>
> Don't question the veracity of what I say. This is a game of fantasy we're playing. We both know it, and reality has no place in it. Quite likely, I'm not telling the truth a lot of the time, and neither are my customers, but that's part of the game, part of what makes it work.

Don't take this all too seriously. Most of all, don't think that we have a personal relationship. We have a business relationship.

In regard to customers, I abide by these rules myself. I don't ask them what they do for a living or how they feel about their divorce. I never question my callers' stories. When someone tells me he has a 16-inch cock, I don't believe it, but I certainly pretend to. That's his fantasy and he has a right to be taken seriously.

The only rule I have about what activities I will "do" in calls is that I won't do anything that doesn't feel right. This might vary with my mood or energy level, but usually it's something that's either too intrusive or too immoral. I have refused, for example, the following:

> Pretend that I am seducing a child I actually know. (I have pretended that the caller was my son, and seduced him.)

> Humiliate some real person in my life, unless it's someone I'm angry at. (I'll humiliate fantasy people, and I have used requests like this to get out my anger at real individuals.)

Beyond this subjective ground rule of only doing what feels okay, however, anything goes in this business. Phone sex is a vehicle for expressing "unacceptable" desires and needs, for exploring feelings and experiences that would be too intense or too painful in real life. It is a way of stretching the limits, going beyond the boundaries of socially acceptable behavior, without hurting anyone.

Whether phone sex actually encourages harmful behaviors is a question for which I don't really have the answer. My hope is that it does not—that, in fact, it prevents such behavior, by giving the same payoffs that the behavior itself would. It certainly does not cure the root cause of these behaviors—the loneliness, inadequacy, fear—although it could help the caller to accept these feelings within himself.

I never feel attacked or put down (or exalted) by the caller, because I know that it's not really me he's talking to, it's his fantasy woman. I'm only a vehicle, and my job is to play that part as best I can.

In spite of the safety of the phone situation, some people are still inhibited. Part of my job is to make them feel safe enough to let down those inhibitions. They're paying to get their needs met, and they can't do that if they don't let their needs be known. I have a couple of ways of helping people to feel safe. The primary one is to match my energy level to the caller's. If he's low-key and quiet, I talk more slowly, with lots of pauses. If he's energetic and enthusiastic, I talk faster, laugh more, am more descriptive. Matching the caller's energy lets him know that it's okay to be whatever he is, to feel whatever he's feeling. This is a technique I learned working on the crisis hotline.

Another way of helping someone feel safe is, as I have mentioned, to be nonjudgmental. Within some very liberal limits, I'll listen to anything and "do" anything. When I respond to "far-out" stories or requests with acceptance and interest, the caller feels safe to share more.

When the caller feels safe, he'll let me know his darkest sexual secrets. I'm not talking about his past exploits—I hear plenty of that, too, and I know most of it's BS. I'm talking about feelings, needs, fantasies. When I'm doing the calls, I often feel that I'm journeying into a dark and hidden country, something like the world of dreams. I'm always watching my own feelings and trying to tune in to the caller's, trying to figure out what's really going on. I hear a lot, participate in a lot, learn a lot. This work continually pushes my limits.

The first thing I learned when I started doing phone sex was that I didn't know nearly as much as I thought I did about sex. This happened the very first night. Out of four calls I did that first evening, two were "non-standard". One was a transvestite and the other wanted me to pretend I was making it with a dog.

Not that I hadn't heard of such things, but I just wasn't prepared for them. I didn't know how to respond to a deep masculine voice telling me, "I'm wearing a red garter belt and black lace hose." Little did I know then that transvestites, no matter how intimidating they may sound, are the most easy-going and friendly of all callers.

As for fucking a dog, since I didn't know any details about this activity, I couldn't lead the caller through the fantasy effectively. Later, I asked a male friend who had also done phone sex how to handle this fantasy. His advice, which I have used ever since when faced with an unfamiliar request, was to ask the caller to describe what's going on. Then I just respond to his initiatives.

So began my graduate-level sex education. On-the-job training, as we say in the business world.

I soon learned, too, that I had to protect myself from the emotional energies of the callers. I simply could not afford to let myself feel all of their pain and intensity. I needed to find a way to stay grounded in myself while still being effective with the callers.

It took some time and practice to detach myself. Some calls evoked a deep compassion in me, some disgusted me. What I figured out eventually was that I needed to tune in to the caller's feelings but not take them on or react to them. When I started doing this, I stopped trying to understand all the callers. I no longer ask myself, "What is this guy trying to work out by harassing me (or by being raped by an animal or obsessed with oversized cocks)?" Calls can still haunt me, just as calls on the crisis hotline can haunt me, but I just accept them instead of analyzing them.

Besides the challenge of learning to handle calls without being over-whelmed, I've found some other rewards. (If I hadn't, I would have dropped out of the business long ago.)

Many people conjecture that it must be rewarding to be giving people pleasure. Actually, though, this is not how I perceive my experiences. If the customer is satisfied, they get off and they're happy, then I've done my job with no complaints, but that doesn't do much for me. I feel that sex without emotional commitment is mostly distraction or compulsion anyway, not really pleasure.

My job satisfaction comes from feeling that I've used my creativity to get through a particularly challenging call, or that I've succeeded in drawing out someone who was reluctant. Perhaps I've evoked a hidden need that the caller had—maybe one he didn't even know he had—and found a way of satisfying that need. I've been surprised sometimes by changes of direction in calls. Perhaps a call that starts out being the standard "hot-and-sexy" type ends up with the caller admitting that he always wanted to be raped by a man, or that he's really obsessed with women's underwear, or that he still fantasizes about making it with his high-school English teacher.

Another reward is entertainment—my own. Granted, most of the calls are boring, but some are entertaining. I always hope I'll get at least one interesting call per evening, and I'm rarely disappointed.

Sometimes I'm amused by a call, and laugh hysterically after I hang up. Although I've never laughed out loud at a caller, there have been times when it was difficult not to. The caller who came the closest to cracking me up was a submissive who told me that he had a special chair he could sit in, with a built-in dildo that popped up at unexpected moments and went up his ass. "Oh, how exciting!" I exclaimed, choking down a guffaw.

Some of the calls are just plain fun, too. People who put out a lot of energy are a joy to work with, whether or not I can relate to their particular fantasy. Sometimes I'm delighted by a call that meshes with my own fantasies.

It's also nice when the customer compliments me on my work, although this is an added bonus and not something I expect or need all the time. I get compliments for being a good actress, for being fun or sensuous, or sometimes just for being effective. Remarks like: "You really helped me out tonight," "I'll sleep well now," "You have a wonderful voice," "You put out good energy," or just "You're wonderful" make me feel great. I like to be appreciated.

Once in a great while, I really get high off a call, and not necessarily in a sexual way. But I can get the same kind of glow from some calls that

I can get from a really exciting sexual encounter—that feeling of float-
ing on air the next day. This can happen without my even getting
physically aroused during the call.

I'll talk in more detail about what kinds of calls can produce this effect
and what I think it's all about. I mention it here because it demonstrates clearly something that I have always believed: that the best
part of sex is in the mind. And that's what phone sex is all about,
really.

A fantasy performer and customer together create a scene and play
out their parts, and the energy they generate can be powerful and re-
juvenating. Actually, this isn't that different from what happens in
real live sex. The human mind and emotions are the fuel that drives
sex, more than the body and its responses.

The art of being a phone sex fantasy performer lies in being able to
tune in to the customer enough to figure out the scene he needs and to
be skillful enough to create that scene and work with the caller's energy.

Because it's the caller's call and only one person's needs are being focused on, the complications of a "normal" two-way encounter are
avoided. And because it's all in the mind, the action moves fast and
freely. There are no obstacles, no encumbrances, except those in the
caller's mind.

Phone sex is pure fantasy, and fantasy is powerful. It works.

3

The Callers

When the office gave me an order for a call, they always told me the type of call requested—hot-and-sexy, dominant, etc. But by the time I'd done about half a dozen calls, I had figured out that what really matters is not the "type" of call, but the personality and energy level of the caller. And this information I can't get until I actually start talking with the caller.

When I think back over the calls I've done, it's individual callers I remember, not "submissives" or "transvestites" or "bisexuals." Some callers are wonderful, some are boring, some make me angry, some have fantasies that are hard for me to deal with. And although I admit that I often have strong negative feelings about a caller, I try to set these feelings aside while I'm actually doing the call. I may curse a caller out after I hang up, but while I'm on the phone with him I try to tune in to what he needs, and to give it to him as well as I am able, without judgment and without holding back. That's what he's paying for, and I feel that I have a commitment to be with him as much as I can—to be present in the call.

This commitment, however, doesn't extend beyond the call. I do have feelings, judgments and opinions about the calls and the callers, and that's basically what this book is all about—my feelings, judgments and opinions.

There is certainly a variety of people using phone sex— people of varying personality types, sexual tastes, and degrees of sophistication and self-esteem. But the characteristic I find myself most concerned with is the energy level of the caller. The type of sexual activity in the call is insignificant compared to the caller's energy level.

When I talk about energy levels, I'm not referring just to the amount of talking a caller does, or to his tone of voice or volume. A quiet caller can sometimes give a lot, and a talkative caller can be so demanding and self-centered that he is a royal pain to work with.

I can usually tell within the first 10 or 15 seconds of the call what the caller's energy level is. I get clues from the tone and volume of his voice, the speed with which he talks, and how he responds to my initial conversation.

About half the callers are moderate- to high-energy types—direct, clear about what they want, and easy to satisfy. The other half are difficult in some way. Although there are various ways in which callers can be difficult, they are always hard to satisfy, and they often leave me feeling used or resentful.

For most calls, I start out by describing my physical characteristics (not accurately, by the way). A low-energy caller will just listen, or he may just say "Uh-huh," as if he's bored with my description and wants to get on with the call. A high-energy caller will give me some feedback—maybe some remarks like, "You sound great," or "I love big nipples," or maybe just moaning.

I try to talk slowly enough so that the caller can interject a question if he wants to. If he does ask a question, I often modify my description to respond. For example, if he asks, "How big are your tits?", I take this as a clue that he would like them to be big, so I give a larger size than my standard. (A man who liked small tits wouldn't ask the question in that way. He would say something like, "I hope your tits aren't too big.")

With dominant calls, I start out by asking if he can tell me what kinds of things he wants. Often I'll get a high-energy submissive who'll tell me exactly what he wants and doesn't want: "I like to get whipped and humiliated and have you punish my balls a lot. I don't like having anything up my ass, and I don't want any men involved."

A low-energy submissive, on the other hand, may just say something like, "I want to be your slave" or "I'll do anything you want." I think, "Great, that's real specific." Submissives like this actually have very specific things they want, but somehow I am supposed to know this, to read their minds. Eventually, during the call, they will let me know what they want, but sometimes I have to drag it out of them. Or I find out what they don't want simply by making mistakes.

"I've got this big dildo here. I'm gonna stick it up your ass."
"No. I don't like things up my ass."
"Oh...okay. Then I'll tie you up."
"No. I don't want to be tied up." (Pause). "Is your boyfriend there?"
"Yes, and he's going to stick his hard cock in your mouth. Suck on it!" (Caller moans).
And this after his saying, "I want you to do anything you want to me."

Most of my callers are easy to work with, although they're dull. They hold no surprises. They do pretty standard calls—nothing very bizarre. The really low-energy types require me to put out more, but at least they are predictable, and I know how to get them off quickly. The callers with just a little higher energy are easier and are really my favorites if I'm low on energy myself and not in the mood for working very hard.

THE QUIET LOW- TO MODERATE-ENERGY CALLER

The really low-energy caller is not really comfortable with his sexuality, doesn't have much imagination and isn't able to give much. Since he doesn't really know what he wants, I usually run my "standard line" for the type of call he has requested. This type of caller is so quiet that I sometimes wonder if he's still there and listening.

It's hard for most people to realize, I think, that the telephone, like radio, only works when you make noise. Silence gives no information. These quiet low-energy callers don't seem to realize that unless they give me feedback with their voices, I have absolutely no idea what's going on with them. I don't know if they're getting aroused, getting close to coming, totally bored, angry ... whatever.

Although this is frustrating, I've learned to put up with it. I'm sure that most of them don't withdraw maliciously; they are just unaware that I can't read their minds. What I do with these callers is to run through my standard line for a few minutes, then ask them something like, "Do you want to come in my mouth?" (if I'm giving them a blow job), "Are you close to coming?" or "What can I do to get you to come?".

Often, they'll just say, "Keep on with what you're doing" or something to that effect. I mentally groan to myself, "Do you have any idea how boring and exhausting this is?", and continue. Mercifully, they usually don't take long to get off. Often they will hang up without even telling me they're done. I'm used to this, and I don't take it personally. I am just relieved when the call is over. If all the calls were like this, I would never have stayed in this business.

Actually, I think that most of these people fall into the "unable to fantasize" category. They just get off on "hot talk." Hearing someone talk graphically about sex excites them enough to come.

I once got a caller like this who, although he wasn't totally silent, would say only "Uh-huh" repeatedly. We had a real exciting conversation. It went something like this:

"Your cock is so hard!"
"Uh-huh."
"Shove that hard cock in my wet pussy!"
"Uh-huh."
"You make me so hot!"
"Uh-huh."
"Can you feel how wet my pussy is?"
"Uh-huh."
"Fuck me deep with that hard cock!"
"Uh-huh."
"Did you come?"
"Uh-huh."

A cut above the super-low-energy callers are those who are more participatory, although not really high-energy. They don't talk much, but they will at least tell me what they want and do a little moaning and groaning. Even though they may not have much imagination, they will carry on a two-way interchange, and make enough noise that I usually know when they've come.

"Would you like to stick that nice hard cock up my wet pussy?"
"I'd like to put it up your ass."
"Oooh, I love it up the ass. Shove it in deep!"
(Caller moans.)
"Can you feel how tight my ass is around your cock?"
"Oh, it's so tight!"
Etc....

In contrast to the "uh-huh" caller, I once got a moderate-energy caller who continually responded "Oh, yeah!" to everything I said:

"Can I suck your cock?"
"Oh, yeah!"
"Would you like to suck on my tits?"
"Oh, yeah!"
"Ooh, that makes my pussy so wet! Would you like to feel it up?"
"Oh, yeah!"

This was a lot easier to work with than "uh-huh."

Moderate-energy callers will usually thank me, even if briefly, at the end of the call, and they don't usually hang up on me.

THE LONELY, BORED OR CURIOUS CALLER

Some guys don't call up phone sex to do sex, really. They'll even admit it. Maybe they got home from work and the house was empty and they're lonely. Or they saw an ad in a porno magazine and were curious about it. So they called up.
These lonely, bored or curious callers are even more of an effort than the quiet, low-energy callers. They put out <u>no</u> energy. None. They

are incredibly draining. Actually, the curious ones are the least drain-ing of the group, because they'll end the call fairly quickly, as soon as they find out what it's about. The lonely or bored ones will go on for their entire time limit, talking about their jobs, their broken relation-ships, their hobbies, etc., etc. I try to push them into getting sexual in hopes of getting them off and moving them on, but I usually can't.

One time I got one of the curious callers and actually grossed him out. Since he wasn't saying much, I just went on with my standard "hot and sexy" line. I figured that he was one of the quiet, low-energy call-ers. When I finally paused to ask him if there was anything more he wanted, he replied with disgust, "No, thank you, I think I've heard enough of this!" Click.

When I first started doing phone sex, one of my greatest fears was that some group of guys at a party would call me up and put me on a speaker phone. Well, like many worst fears, this one came true. However, only one guy answered the phone, and he didn't tell me what was going on at first. I started running my standard "hot-and-sexy" line, but his attention just didn't seem to be there. He kept laughing—not the usual reaction, to say the least. I knew something was going on, but I just put it down to his being weird. Finally, he admitted that he was with a bunch of guys listening in on a speaker phone, and I started laughing too.

Actually, I didn't feel that bad about it, once it had happened. I didn't take it personally. They were just curious and probably a little drunk.

THE DEMANDING CALLER

Callers can be demanding in a number of ways. They can be angry and abusive. They can demand a great variety of activities or ask a lot of intrusive questions. Or they may be drunk or just be extremely low-energy types who contribute almost nothing to the call.

I have mixed feelings about these callers. Some of them can be inter-esting because they are so bizarre. Yet they require the most energy of any type, and they can leave me feeling tired and used. Often, after I say my cordial "good night and call me again" line, I hang up and curse them out.

The extremely low-energy callers (I call them zero-energy types) are the most trying for me. I have to keep up a constant monologue; they won't even answer a direct question:

"Let me take that hard cock in my mouth and suck on it. Ooh, that tastes so good! Let me suck it into my throat! Can you feel how wet my mouth is on your cock?" (Silence.) "Let me sit on that hard cock! Oh, it's so deep and hard inside me! You make me so wet! Let me squeeze your cock with my pussy. Can you feel that?" (Silence.) "What can I do to get you to come?" (Silence.) "I'm riding your cock so hard! Feel how hot your cock is getting! I can feel it so deep inside me, opening my pussy up! I want to feel your cum in my pussy!" (Pause.) "Did you come?" (Silence.)

I feel as though I'm pouring energy into a black hole.

Eventually, they hang up. They might even say good-bye—usually the only thing I hear from them, after their first few words at the beginning of the call.

Just a little higher-energy are drunks. I have very little to say about drunks, and none of it is good. They can't get it up, they can't get off, and they never take any responsibility for this behavior: it's supposed to be my fault for not arousing them enough. (Give me a break.) They have no imagination, they use up their entire time limit, and they are ungrateful. If I never talked to another one again, it wouldn't be too soon. Sometimes I get lucky and they accidentally unplug the phone during the call. More often, I think they pass out, or come close to it.

I do calls with drunks only because I figure I have to pay a few dues in return for the good calls I get. I feel that they are wasting my time, but since they're paying customers, I have to put up with a few of them.

The more abusive types of overly demanding callers are the ones who are angry—at women, at life and really, I think, at themselves. Like the drunks, these guys rarely get off. They have used sex to express their anger for so long that they are burned out on it. Sex no longer stimulates them. They deny this fact, however, and try to compensate for it by getting more and more bizarre stimulation.

Most of these callers want a submissive. They're into punishing; they want to hear pain, screaming, sobbing and self-degradation from the performer:

"No, please! Don't shove your cock so deep in my ass!"
"Shut up, you bitch!"
(Sobbing) "You hurt my ass so bad! You're splitting my ass open! Please, stop it!"
"You're just a no-good whore! You need to get fucked in the ass, don't you?!"
"Yes, I do! I'm a whore and a slut! Fuck me harder!"
Et cetera...

I don't mind a little of this, since it at least gives me a chance to do some acting, but because they don't get off, I have to go on and on. Like the quiet, low-energy call, this one gets old fast. Also, screaming makes me hoarse, which is not good for doing subsequent calls.

In spite of the abusive content of this type of call, though, it is mildly interesting. I am intrigued by how bizarre they can get sometimes, and wonder what is really going on in their heads. I think that they just get a kick (and not necessarily a sexual one) out of abusing someone.

These callers usually ask for a "kinky" call and want me to do some of the more unusual sexual activities—getting fucked by male animals (orally, anally, vaginally, or some combination), eating shit, or being beaten and gang-raped. More important than the activities, though, are my responses. They need to know that they are hurting someone.

These are the callers who, more than any other, make me feel that I'm descending a long staircase into the depths of the underworld. This sensation doesn't scare me, since I know I'll get out as soon as the call is over. But I wonder if the caller gets out. These calls leave me with a poignant feeling, which can last a long time after the call is over. Whenever the memory comes back to me, I ask myself, "Did I really do all that stuff? What kind of a world am I living in?"

This type of caller, however, is rare. I've done only a few dozen of them in the years I've been working.

Another kind of demanding caller is the one who keeps up a constant barrage of questions:

"What's the kinkiest thing you ever did?"
"What's the biggest cock you ever had?"
"Have you ever made it with a woman?"
"Do you have a dildo?"

I start out playing these calls straight, taking them seriously and trying to give them what they want. But if the call progresses and continues to be unfocused, I often try to gross these guys out, just to see how they'll respond. For my material I use a lot of stuff from the blatantly angry calls. But often they don't seem to really hear anything I'm saying. It's not unusual for them to ask the same question more than once during the call. Or they may interrupt my spiel with a totally unrelated question:

"When's the first time you made it with another woman?"
"About three years ago, with my best girlfriend."
"Tell me about how that happened."
"Well, we were sitting and talking about how we both wanted to see what it was like to be with a woman. Then we started kissing, and I put my hand inside her blouse and started feeling up her tits. They were so soft! I could feel her nipples getting hard..."
"What's the biggest cock you ever had?"

"About twelve inches. It was this big black guy that I picked up in a bar. When I got him home and got his pants off, I couldn't believe how big it was. I started getting hot just looking at it. I ..."
"Do you have a vibrator?"
"Absolutely. I never leave home without it."

THE INVASIVE CALLER

The invasive caller is the only one that I experience as abusive, and mercifully they are rare. These are the people who want me to participate in the call in the same way that they do. They want to be sure I am masturbating also, that I am going to get off with them.

What feels most invasive about this type is that they ask me a lot of detailed questions about myself—my body, my sexual tastes, what exactly I'm doing to myself right now. I don't, of course, tell the truth, but their intrusiveness requires me to keep up a constant stream of lies. This can be exhausting, and I come away feeling used and intruded on.

"Are you playing with your pussy?"
"Oh, yes! I've got two fingers in my pussy, and I'm stroking them in and out, getting it real wet."
"Let me hear it."
"Sure. I'll put the phone down there and you can hear it." (I won't go into my sound-effect techniques, but suffice it to say that for these situations I have some.) "Can you hear how wet it is?"
"Yeah. Are your nipples hard?"
"Yes, they're so hard! I'm squeezing them, getting them real hard. It makes me so hot when I play with my nipples!"

Another way that callers are sometimes invasive is by asking me personal questions, such as what I do with my boyfriend, how old I was when I lost my virginity, what my favorite position is, etc. I try to divert these questions by focusing back on them:

"What's your favorite thing to do?"
"Oh, I like all kinds of things. What would you like to do tonight?"

If he's persistent I'll make something up.

I feel that these invasive callers are breaking the rules of phone sex. One of my major rules is that I do not participate or make myself vulnerable in the calls. I am an actress, a professional. That's why I get paid and they don't. It's their needs that are getting met.

I think that these guys need for me to come down to their level. They always sound depressed, even resentful, and I think they want me to be down there with them, in order to validate their feelings. As one of them told me, "I don't want to be doing this by myself." I don't feel I am obligated, or even able, to provide that kind of validation. There are limits to phone sex, and this is one of them. These callers, like the demanding ones, take themselves entirely too seriously.

THE PARTICIPATORY CALLER

This is the caller who makes the job worthwhile. They know what they want and they ask for it. I do it, and they get off. They always thank me, often give me compliments, say they'll call me again, which they often do. They are not extremely quiet, extremely loud, extremely demanding, or extremely anything. They give and they take. They are good to work with.

Some participatory callers are so high-energy that I categorize them as "sensuous." These guys are great. They love sex, they are proud of their bodies, and they share themselves joyfully. They ask for a lot of energy from me, but they give a lot in return.

Although this type is more common in the sensuous dominant call, it is not limited to it. Some of my sensuous dominant calls do not involve sensuous callers and some sensuous callers do other types of calls.

These callers invite me to participate in the call, but not in the same way as the invasive or demanding callers. The sensuous caller never questions what I am really doing, never demands to know.

He doesn't need to take me to where he is; he is happy there and complete in himself. The sensuous caller tells me, in effect, "I'm wonderful and I want to share myself with you." The invasive or demanding caller tells me, "I need for you to tell me that I am wonderful."

The sensuous callers are the most verbal of all my callers. Sometimes they describe the setting—the room, the bed, their bodies—in such graphic detail, with such enthusiasm, that I find myself getting caught up in the call in spite of myself.

"I'm lying here on my king-size bed. There's a fire in the fireplace and I'm lying here naked. Come sit on the bed beside me. Let me look at your beautiful body."
"I'm sitting on the bed beside you, showing off my tits to you. See how round and firm they are?"
"Your tits are beautiful!"
"See how hard my nipples are?"
"God, they're beautiful! My cock is so hard for you! Look at it sticking straight up in the air!"
"I want it! Let me take it in my hand and feel how warm it is!"
"Your hand is so soft!"
"I want to taste your cock, flick my tongue over it..."

And off we go. I often tell these guys that they should be phone sex performers themselves.

REGULAR CUSTOMERS

Regular clients are the bread and butter of any business, and phone sex is no exception. When I worked for the service, I didn't have as much ability to build up a regular clientele as I do now that I'm on my own. If I wasn't working on the night they called, they might take someone else. Now, if they don't get me, they have to go to the trouble of finding another service, which they may or may not do.

I also have more control over who my clients are, now that I have my own service, by the way I advertise. I tend to get more of the imaginative, sensuous callers that I love to work with, and they are more likely to become regulars because I provide the quality they're looking for. I'm also better at setting boundaries now, so I don't feel intruded on by regulars who call me when I'm not working, which was sometimes a problem in the early years.

Among my regulars have been two doctors, a Protestant minister, and an investigator for a federal regulatory agency (no, not the IRS). The doctors spent a lot of time trying to impress me, the minister liked to confide in me, especially about his sexual exploits, as he didn't have much opportunity to do that with anyone in his "real" life. I think the federal regulator died. (One thing you have to learn to deal with in the sex business is that no one ever notifies you when your clients die.)

One of the doctors was the most interesting but saddest case. He was obsessed with oversized cocks; he practically worshipped them. (He was the one who sent me the dildo that I donated to the phone sex office). He was looking for a woman with a large enough capacity to take a big cock and with the same obsession herself. With my excellent acting skills, I of course convinced him that I was such a person, even though on my second call with him I had to be reminded of what it was I was obsessed with. He was a heavy user of pornography that featured large cocks and dildoes, and he loved to fantasize about watching me get fucked with huge dildoes. "See how wide my pussy stretches?" I would brag. "Oh, my God, oh my God," he would gasp, almost losing his voice. "I can't believe how big and beautiful your cunt is!"

He wanted a lot of humiliation for not being exceptionally endowed himself. The first time I talked to him, he told me his own cock was eight inches long. Several calls later he admitted, sobbing, that it was really only six, and then later still he shortened it to five-and-a-half. After he sent me some photographs of himself in the nude, fully erect (I donated these to a gay male friend, who was delighted with them), I realized that the shorter versions must refer to his flaccid length. He was so determined to be inadequate that he had to compare his non-erect length to the oversized cocks he saw on exceptionally well-endowed men!

Over time, I felt that our calls were getting more and more bizarre. I would alternate between exclaiming over how much I loved big cocks and laughing at his normal-sized one, taunting him for not even being able to excite me: "It would take ten of your cocks for me to even feel anything inside me!" He assured me that he would feel privileged to be allowed to satisfy me by operating a dildo himself, or by fisting me (putting his whole fist and part of his forearm into my vagina). Of course he was not worthy of fucking me directly. I would have him fantasize a scenario where he went into a lingerie store and bought some women's panties for himself (he had a collection already), telling the teenage salesgirl that they were for him and that no, he didn't need a larger size. She would laugh and demand to see his inadequate cock, then tell him that her 11-year-old brother was better endowed than he. This fantasy would invariably get him off in a big way. "I shot my cum three or four feet across the room!" he would exclaim.

He bragged to me that he had sexually harassed some male patients at the prison where he worked (I have since found out that prison is where the most incompetent doctors end up), demanding that the better-endowed ones drop their pants so that he could "see if everything is okay down there." He eventually got his comeuppance, however, when he encountered a real-life super-hung inmate who ganged up with one of the guards and started sexually harassing him in return. They raped him anally and demanded that he perform anilingus on both of them, rewarding him with brief glimpses and touches of the amazing cock.

He was a sad case, and not very bright. It was hard for me to believe that anyone with his obviously limited mental capacity could have gotten through medical school. I continued doing calls with him because I felt sorry for him, but I also felt helpless to do anything constructive for him. He was a strange mixture of submissive, transvestite and obsessive.

For a while I thought his only problem was that he was gay and couldn't deal with it, but I eventually came to believe that he had some heavier-duty stuff going on as well. His willingness to put up with abuse and his feelings of inadequacy for being normal-sized were probably indications that he had suffered some kind of abuse as a child. He never got around to dealing with this, though, at least not that I'm aware of.

. . . . .

The callers, more than the type of call, make phone sex what it is. I am fascinated by their differing energy levels and perceptions—of themselves, of me, of sex. I am amazed at the variety of approaches that people use to pursue the same goal—sexual gratification.

Although I struggle to deal successfully with the low-energy callers, even in these struggles I learn something. I am often surprised and gratified to discover the depth of my own capacity—my flexibility, my open-mindedness, my acting ability. My willingness to go with the call, wherever the caller wants it to go, has led me into places I never dreamed of. My callers have taken me on these journeys.

4

The Standard Types of Calls

Although as I have already said, the type of call is less important than the energy level of the caller, categorizing calls by type is the easiest way for me to describe my phone sex experiences. But I have my own categorization system, different from the official categories that the service used.

The specified category that the service gave me was a starting point for the call. Even when it was accurate, however, this category was at best just an approximation of what the customer wanted. Each type of call can vary with the callers' energy levels, personalities and degrees of sexual sophistication.

And I learned not to assume that the category I was given with the order was going to be the "real" category. A lot of customers didn't understand the categories, particularly if they were first-time callers. The people who answered the phones in the office often rattled off the categories so quickly that the customer probably couldn't even hear them, much less understand them. So I got a lot of confused callers, and I learned that I had to clarify what the customer really wanted.

Some guys would ask for a dominant, for example, without having the faintest idea what that meant. They may have thought that it just meant an aggressive woman. I had a couple of callers who asked for a lesbian when what they wanted was a dominatrix. To many people, "kinky" just means "uninhibited." To a more sophisticated customer, it may mean golden showers (urinating on someone), sex with animals, or something else out of the ordinary.

So before I launched into a full-fledged performance, I always checked out what the caller really wanted. Usually I would just ask if he had any special requests. With dominant orders, I generally asked

"How dominant do you want?" or "What kinds of things would you like me to do?" From their response, I could tell whether they really knew what dominant meant. (If they did, they would be specific, or would at least say something like "I want to be your slave." If they didn't know what dominant meant, they'd be vague: "What do you want me to do to you tonight?" "Oh, I don't know. I just need some help getting off.")

The "Standard" Call

When I worked for a phone-sex service, about three quarters of my calls fell into this category. The caller was usually one of the three most common types—quiet, with either low or moderate energy, or moderately participatory. I would, however, get a few sensuous callers in this category.

The category that the service would specify with the order for this type of call was either "hot and sexy," "kinky" or "dominant." These were the callers who didn't know what "kinky" or "dominant" really meant. The real category was always "hot and sexy."

After giving my (imaginary) physical description, I would ask the caller if he had anything particular he wanted me to do. The answer was almost invariably something like "Oh, whatever you want," "I just want us to have a good time," or "I want you to be kinky" (whatever that meant).

A sensuous caller, though, would respond with something more intense, like "I want you to drive me crazy," "I want to drive you crazy," or "I want to enjoy every inch of you." He might elaborate on exactly what he did want to do: "I want you to tease me for a while, and then I want to beg you to let me eat your pussy."

Now I knew what type of caller I had, and I could change my approach to suit his needs. For the lower-energy callers, I'd run my standard line. With the higher-energy caller, we might talk for a while about what his preferences were and how he wanted these things done. After that, the call took off without much more effort on my part.

Now that I have my own service, I don't have anyone to preview the type of call for me. I ask the customer directly and specifically what he wants; I don't offer him a category. Since I advertise myself as being a sort of specialist in out-of-the-ordinary calls, though, I get very few "standard" callers. The few I do get are mostly guys who just like my voice (of which I have a sample on my website).

My standard line for lower-energy callers is basically just my own style. It may not be the best approach, but it works. I start out by asking what he's doing right now: is he in bed, naked, sitting at the kitchen table smoking, or on the couch watching TV. (I refuse to do calls when the caller has the TV on during the call, unless he's watching a porno show. I ask him to turn it off. Otherwise, I'd feel that I was competing with the TV the whole time, and it's difficult to get somebody off when you don't have their full attention.)

If he is naked, I ask if I can fondle him. If he's not naked, I ask if I can undress him. This is sometimes how I find out that he's a cross dresser:

"Are you naked?"
"No, I'm wearing white lace panties and a pink teddy."
"Oh."
If I discover that he's a cross dresser, I then switch into my standard transvestite line.

If he's a low-to-moderate-energy, non-transvestite caller, I usually control the call from this point on. Oral sex is popular, both ways. Anal sex is also amazingly popular. In fact, I used to wonder why these guys need a woman at all, since my most popular activities—blow jobs and ass-fucking—could be done with a man just as well. But it finally dawned on me that being straight or gay is more than just wanting a particular type of physical stimulation. It's a matter of which gender of person you feel drawn to and want attention from.

If the action seems to bog down, I throw in a question or suggestion: "Is there anything else you'd like to do to me?" "Can I taste your cock?" "Would you like to put that hard cock between my soft tits?" If they're a moderate-energy caller, they may take advantage of these interjections to request an alternative: "No, I'd like to put it in your pussy," for example. If they're a really low-energy caller, they may not respond at all, even to a direct question. This doesn't faze me: I just keep going. Some people get tongue-tied when they have to talk about sex.

These callers usually get off in about five to seven minutes, unless they're drunk. These are short, easy and boring calls, but I don't mind them, particularly if I'm not in the mood to put out much energy myself. I think I could do one of these calls in my sleep, although I've never tried it.

The sensuous callers who want a standard call, however, are an entirely different story. Even though they may not come up with any particularly original activities, they put so much energy into what they do that they can make the most mundane sexual activities seem exciting. They verbalize a lot—moaning, groaning and exclaiming: "You taste so good!" "My cock is so hard!" "I love to feel your pussy juices on my face!"

One of my most memorable calls was a standard hot-and-sexy with a sensuous caller. It was his birthday, and he wanted to top off the day with a hot phone call. We had a great time together even though we didn't do anything out of the ordinary.

Sensuous callers, though, are more likely to get into some of the less common activities, such as rimming (ass licking) or golden showers. This isn't because they're really kinky or demanding but simply because they're adventurous. But even without any of the "trimmings," I can come away from a call with a sensuous caller feeling really energized.

THE PSEUDO-INTIMATE CALL

This is one of the most difficult calls for me to deal with. These callers want our encounter to be intimate and meaningful rather than just fun. They want foreplay—kissing, caressing, massaging, whispered endearments. To play this part well, I have to act emotionally involved rather than just sexually aroused. I often feel like a con artist, deceitful, calloused and manipulating, while the caller seems to be vulnerable, tender and caring. It's hard for me to keep up my own self-esteem with this type of call. I have to remind myself that he's actually being manipulative and needy, not tender and caring. I feel intruded on: I need to save tenderness and affection for my own relationships. Keeping them out of phone sex gives me some measure of privacy and is one of the ways I keep sane on this job.

I was surprised at first to find myself having these reactions. When I fantasized about doing phone sex, before I actually started doing it, I imagined that I would be delighted to find this kind of caller. What I was doing in these fantasies, however, was confusing intimacy with sensuality. They are not the same thing.

The sensuous caller is giving, and he enjoys sex for its own sake. He has no illusions about the level of sharing that we are participating in during the call. He knows that it's fantasy, that it's here and now, and nothing more or less. The pseudo-intimate caller, though, doesn't perceive that phone sex is fantasy. He expects a lot more from the call than can be achieved. He wants meaning and connection. Although there is a certain intimacy in the phone sex call, it's not the kind he's thinking of. It's a transitory, limited intimacy, based on sharing a few minutes of sexual games.

One time when I was visiting the phone sex office I got a request call, and it turned out to be one of these pseudo-intimate guys. Unfortunately, although they gave me a private room to do the call, I couldn't figure out the phone system, so I ended up doing the call from a pay phone in the hall. Since it was late at night, I was lucky enough not to get any cross traffic, but I was pissed off at having to do one of these calls in this situation. I kept thinking, "Cut the crap, honey, just get off and let me get out of here."

The worst example of this type of call is when a repeat customer starts to develop an emotional attachment to me. This has happened only a few times, but it is really irritating when it does happen. I have to struggle to keep the boundaries clear while still trying to perform according to the contract that I feel I have with the caller.

What's really going on for me with this type of call, I think, is that my needs are at odds with the caller's. I need to be detached and businesslike, to hold myself apart from the action. He needs to feel connected with another human being, and all that I can offer him is a pretense. I feel sad about not being able to fulfill all his needs, but I'm also resentful because he is expecting more of me than I am committed to giving. These guys are actually invasive callers. They need for me to be at the same level they are, and I'm not. Nor should I be.

THE BISEXUAL CALL

I enjoy doing bisexual calls because I am somewhat attracted to women and consequently find it easy to play that role, but these calls are really not much different from standard "hot and sexy" calls. They seem a little more relaxing and enjoyable than the "hot and sexy," but perhaps this is only because I do them less frequently.

There are two types of bisexual calls: two women and a man, and two men and a woman. (There can also be multiple men and women, but these are generally dominant calls, not bisexual.) The most common is the two-woman/one-man combination. In my experience, this has always been me with an imaginary woman, not with another performer.

Usually, the caller wants to watch me make it with another woman. He either watches for the entire time (i.e., until he gets off) or, more commonly, at some point he joins the action. Occasionally, he just needs to watch long enough to get aroused, and then the other woman disappears and he makes it with me alone. At that point, the call switches to a standard "hot and sexy" call.

Sometimes the caller wants to be part of a two-man/one-woman *menage a' trois*. Or he may want me to tell about a time when I participated in such an encounter. These calls can be a lot of fun, since there are more possibilities of what you can do with three people than with just two.

I should mention here that for my imaginary third parties in calls I usually use real people that I know—their real first names and physical descriptions. This has several advantages over trying to conjure up imaginary people: it's less effort and it allows me to indulge some of my own fantasies, while not detracting in any way from the call. And it certainly makes it easier for me to describe these people and to answer any questions the caller may have. I don't have to remember what lies I made up.

I make an exception to this practice if the caller asks for a specific type of person (e.g., a five-foot-two willowy blonde with small tits) and I don't have anyone in my acquaintance who fits the description. When this happens, though, the caller generally has someone in mind himself.

Occasionally, a caller will want to drop me from the call altogether and make it with an imaginary man. He needs me only to direct the call—tell him what to do, what the man is doing to him, etc.

I'm not sure what this type of call is about. I never know whether the caller planned to get into gay sex before he called, or whether he became aware of that need as the call progressed. I suspect the latter, simply because there are plenty of phone sex lines available for gay men. There may be something going on here about needing permission from a woman to indulge in gay sex, or just needing a woman to get started with because that's more comfortable for a straight man. It could also be an expression of anger against women—making me watch but not letting me participate— but that's not my take on this type of call. I have never heard any anger directed at me during these calls.

One time I did get a real gay call. A man called me from a hotel room where he was in the process of getting it on with another man. Somehow, he needed me as a facilitator, to let it be okay for him to go ahead and make it with this man. This caller asked for a bisexual call, and he didn't reveal what he really wanted until several minutes into the call. The call did seem unfocused, and I knew something was not clicking, but I couldn't figure out what it was. When he finally told me, I asked him a few questions to clarify exactly what was happening: Was this the first time that he had ever been sexual with a man? Answer: yes. I validated his feelings of being scared and unsure of what to expect. Were they both undressed? Had they been fondling each other? Were they both hard? I then suggested that he let the other man suck his cock, and I told him to concentrate on how good it felt: "Feel how wet his mouth is, feel his tongue licking your cock." It didn't take long for him to come.

Although I never spoke to the other man, I sincerely believe that this was a truthful call. The clues I picked up were the caller's hesitancy in telling me what was going on, the fear in his voice, and the intensity with which he came. A blow job is much more intense stimulation than masturbation.

This call was an experience I will always treasure. I have known several gay people who didn't get in touch with their sexual orientation until well into their adulthood, and I have seen what a freeing experience that realization can be. I felt honored to be a part of that experience for someone and to provide a validation for his feelings that he seemed to need at that time. This seemed more like a crisis-line call than a phone-sex call.

THE ANGRY SUBMISSIVE CALL

The dominant/submissive terminology may be confusing, since I use it to refer both to calls and to callers. Phone sex workers refer to calls by the role that the performer plays, not by the role the caller plays. So when I talk about a submissive call, I mean that I am the submissive, not the caller. Someone who requests a submissive call is not a submissive but a dominant.

Most angry submissive calls are easy, once the real action starts. All I have to do is respond, and the responses are usually fun to act out—sobbing, screaming, begging for mercy or saying degrading things about myself ("I am such a slut, whore, pig ... I need to get fucked in the ass..." etc.). I don't feel degraded by these activities because I can hear how much the caller needs me to say and do these things. It's obvious that he's very dependent on me to provide these stimuli—he needs them to get off. His neediness gives me power over him.

There are two basic types of angry dominants. The first is the honest one: he knows what he wants, and he asks for a submissive when he places his order. The other type usually asks for a "kinky." This is usually an angry, demanding caller, who wants me to do all kinds of bizarre things. And he wants me to think them up; he contributes very little energy to the call.

The honest dominant is a participatory caller. He puts out lots of energy. This feels good to me; it's relaxing, and strangely enough, it feels safe. I'm not really being abused, I'm acting a part, and the caller appreciates my effort.

These callers are usually very expressive. Unlike the angry demanding caller, the honest dominant is in touch with his anger. He has figured out that this is a way of directing that anger, which works for him. Since he's in touch with these feelings he's easy to work with.

Once I did a submissive call with a man who told me at the beginning of the call that he was angry at a woman he worked with and wanted to use the call to get out this anger. We worked together on this, and it was an intense, high-energy call. We were both surprised at the level of violence that he came out with. He really got into beating me, verbally abusing me ("You dirty slut!" "You filthy

pig!" "Tell me how much you deserve to be hurt!"), and fantasizing
ripping this woman's labia apart. Yet it was a cleansing experience
for him. It really helped with his anger. I felt that he was one of the
healthiest customers I have ever talked to. It was an intense experience for me, too, leaving me feeling drained but happy.

Another call along these same lines gave me a chance to work out
some of my own anger. This caller at first wanted to abuse me, then
wanted me to participate with him in abusing three other women.
This caller, however, didn't have anyone real in mind; I got to pick
the three women. It so happened that I was involved in a difficult
situation at my daytime job, where I was being harassed by a clique
of three women, so of course I used these women as the imaginary
participants in the call. I had a great time, beating them, smearing
shit all over them, raping them in the ass with dildoes—all the usual
dominant stuff. I felt a lot better after I got done with the call. I also
realized that I needed to get away from that situation, and the next
day started working on transferring to another department.

These honest submissive calls can be rewarding and entertaining.
People who are in touch with their feelings are always easy to work
with.

As for the angry demanding callers, I have talked about them some
already under "Callers." These guys want to involve me in degrading activities too, but they seem to need these more for their self-
validation than for their satisfaction or release from sexual tension.
Because they are demanding, they require more energy, at least at
the beginning of the call, than the honest dominants.

These callers will usually start off by putting the burden of the call
on me. They may ask something like, "What's the kinkiest thing
you can think of?" This is a question I hate. It puts all the responsibility on me to think of something when I have no idea what they
want (maybe they don't, either, of course). I usually answer a question like this by talking about golden showers or even shitting on
someone. This is almost always bizarre enough to satisfy them. If
it's not I can talk about eating shit or forcing someone else to. Or I

can talk about making it with animals or being raped by several men at once (orally, vaginally, anally, maybe with some others thrown in to pee on me or masturbate into my face).

Once the call gets going, the caller will usually put more energy into it. Then it gets a little easier for me and becomes more like the call with an honest dominant.

Often these callers will want me to be subservient to them, to worship them. This isn't the sensuous kind of body worship but a degrading subservience.

"Who do you serve?" one of them asked me. Not sure exactly what he wanted, I asked him.
"You serve my dick," he replied.
"Your dick is my master," I responded. "Let me taste it, please!"
"Call me 'sir'," he ordered me. "And beg for it."
"Please sir, let me taste your dick! I need it so bad!" I wondered if he was a career military man.

These guys need a lot of pain and degradation from me. Once we settle on some activities (oral and anal sex are the most popular), these are pleasant enough calls. I get to practice my acting, and after he gets aroused, he will put out enough energy to keep the call going. But I do come away feeling that I have walked a path of darkness, and I wonder what kind of a world he lives in most of the time.

Some dominant callers want me to tell them a story about a degrading incident, usually a gang rape, that I experienced. Often, they want me to have a boyfriend with me. The boyfriend tries to protect me from the rapists, but he ends up being raped also. These calls are fun. I get to be inventive and even outrageous sometimes. Often these callers are participatory rather than demanding.

There are also many calls that turn submissive part way through the call. I call these "switch-over calls" and they're intriguing to me. The call will start out being a standard "hot and sexy" call. Suddenly, in the midst of fucking, the caller will start saying things like, "You whore! Filthy slut!" I pick this up and run with it. "I'm such a slut! I need to get fucked so bad!" Sometimes the caller switches back, just as abruptly, into standard hot-and-sexy stuff. I switch back with him, never missing a beat. This is one of those situations where you need flexibility.

If the call switches more than two or three times, though, it becomes unfocused. Then I usually ask if there's something I can do to help him get off. He will generally come up with something. If not, the call usually ends with the time limit.

Angry submissive calls can be interesting, once they get focused. But they are rarely sensuous calls. They are not my favorites, but they are not the worst either.

THE SENSUOUS SUBMISSIVE CALL

The stereotype of dominants is that they are angry and violent people, but not all of them are. Some, in fact, can be downright sensuous. Usually these are the ones who are into spanking or bondage, as opposed to beating and abuse. I had one regular caller like this, and he was wonderful. He spent a lot of time at the beginning, taking off my pants, telling me what a great ass I have and what a good time he was going to have spanking me. It was very erotic.

I once got a call from an Englishman (accent and all) who was into caning. ("You know what we do to naughty girls in England?") He was also great fun. The next day, I went in to work at my "regular" job, where I worked with an English guy. I went around all day smirking to myself, thinking, "I know what you do when you go home at night." This was one of those calls that left me feeling high for days afterwards.

Sensuous submissive calls, in short, are great fun, relaxing and entertaining. Unfortunately, they are few and far between. Much more common is ...

THE STRICT OR HEAVY DOMINANT CALL

Like most beginners at phone sex, I didn't do dominant calls when I first started because I felt that sadism was just not a part of my make-up. I didn't even think I could act it convincingly.

Then one night I got a caller who asked for someone to humiliate him, rather than asking for a "dominant." This I felt I could relate to. He had a story fantasy he wanted me to play out. As I listened to his description of his request, I started getting caught up in it. I did the call, I did it well, I got high off it. This was the beginning of my adventure with dominant calls.

This particular caller wanted me to be his mother and to punish him—not an uncommon theme in dominant calls, although usually it is not so blatant. Most submissives don't talk about their mothers in the call. They just want to be dominated by a woman.

Generally, submissives want to be spanked or whipped, fucked in the ass with various objects (dildoes, hot curling irons, etc.), have their genitals punished, be taken to some public place like a party, humiliated, and forced to beg for more abuse (or sometimes to beg for mercy). A common theme is for them to be raped, either orally or anally or both, by other men—frequently the stereotypical well-endowed African-ancestry man. Dominant calls frequently involve group sex situations—being humiliated by just one person is not enough.

When I first started doing phone sex, one of my friends surmised that it must be rewarding to enhance people's self-esteem. That seemed reasonable to me until I started doing dominant calls. I felt that I was doing just the opposite—attacking the callers' self-esteem. Yet they seemed to crave all of the abuse and degradation I could dish out.

The dynamic that's going on here is tricky, yet it makes sense once you understand it. One of my friends who did a lot of real live S and M put it very well: "There's nothing as selfish as a submissive."

The submissive is the center of attention. It may be negative attention, but it is attention.

The submissive also soaks up a lot of energy from his dominant. I noticed this the first time I got a submissive who said, "I want you to do whatever you want to me."

"Well, what kinds of things do you like to have done to you?" I asked.
"Anything you want to do," he replied. "Whatever you want to do to me, I want you to do it."

I felt like saying, "What the hell makes you think I want to do anything to you, anyway? All I want to do is get this call over with and get paid for it. Who do you think you are, that I should sit around dreaming up things to do to you?"

Instead, I said, "Well, I'm going to start out by spanking you. Crawl over to me and stick your ass up in the air."
"Yes, Mistress."

After we got going, he did come up with some suggestions. But it took some time and effort, and I still felt resentful. I'm not, after all, a real dominant.

This passive aggression is not uncommon for submissives. Although the submissive may claim that he wants only to be abused, to be a slave, he actually has very specific ways in which he wants to be abused. Thus he is really the one in control of the fantasy. He is also in control of the dominant, since he has her full attention and energy, especially when he can keep her guessing what he wants. And control is the key word for submissives.

Fortunately, though, most submissives are more direct about their need for control. They will volunteer information about what kind of abuse they want. When I have to find out by ordering someone to do something and having him refuse, it gets tricky, because often one of the dynamics of the dominant call is having the submissive beg for mercy. Yet, there is a difference in the tone of voice when the caller actually refuses to do something, as opposed to begging me to stop while really wanting me to continue. When he refuses, he steps out of his submissive role for a time and just says, quietly and deliberately, "No, that's not my bag," or something to that effect. When he is begging for mercy as part of his submissive role, he protests loudly and vehemently: "No, Mistress, not that! Please don't make me do that!"

Once I got a sensuous submissive caller who asked for specific types of abuse by saying things like, "Oh, no! You're going to make me suck his cock, aren't you?!" "Yes," I replied, "and you'd better swallow every drop of his cum or you'll get another whipping!" Of course he failed in this task and got the promised punishment.

As I did more dominant calls, I developed a standard dominant line to use for unimaginative callers. I start out by spanking and whipping him, progress to fucking him in the ass with a dildo (sometimes I strap it onto myself and sometimes I just hold it in my hand), then have him turn around so that I can whip his genitals. I usually end up ordering him to masturbate with sandpaper. This last activity is invariably popular and almost always gets him off, especially when I exhort him to squeeze tighter, or I fuck him up the ass at the same time.

I have a few extra activities I can throw in if I'm feeling energetic or if the caller seems to need more stimulation. These include putting clamps on his nipples, having him immerse his genitals in boiling water, dripping hot wax on them, and placing rubber bands around the base of his penis or scrotum (he can remove these when he's ready to get serious and come). I can also order him to come in his own face, if that's physically possible, and to be sure and swallow his own cum.

It's usually more stimulating if the caller abuses himself, rather than my doing all the abusing. Even better is to make him tell me how much he deserves this pain and humiliation: "I deserve to have my cock hurt, Mistress. Please hurt it some more!"

Usually the caller only fantasizes that he is being abused. Occasionally, though, I will get a caller who really performs the acts that I order him to do. I go a little easier with these guys. Obviously, one of the ground rules of phone sex is not to cause any real physical harm to the caller.

Once I got a caller who wanted to stick something up his ass but wanted me to tell him what to use. I suggested all of the standard items—dildo, curling iron, hairbrush handle. He had none of these items on hand, however. I found it hard to believe that someone wouldn't have a hairbrush, but he claimed he didn't. Finally, I suggested a broomstick. This he had (I guess he sweeps the floor but doesn't brush his hair). As he went off to get the broom, I thought, "Oh, no! What if it's one of those metal broom handles that has a triangle at the top to hang it up by?!" Evidently it wasn't, however, because it seemed to work with no difficulty.

Another time I got a caller who wanted me not only to abuse him during the call but also to order him to do things the next day. So I told him to go into a supermarket, approach a woman, pull down his pants and ask her to spank him. I assumed that this scenario was one that he would fantasize, not actually do, but I did have visions of a newspaper headline the next day: "FLASHER IN SUPERMARKET ASKS WOMAN FOR SPANKING."

Since I usually end my "normal" calls by thanking the caller for a good time and suggesting he call again, I wasn't sure at first just how to end the dominant calls. I thought maybe I should act like Oscar the Grouch, and say something like, "Have a terrible night! And don't ever call again!" Actually, however, after the caller has come, he switches back into normal consciousness and is perfectly civil, so I end these calls in the same way as the others.

I'm always looking for new material to use in my dominant calls. Once I was in a business meeting at my other job with someone who was talking about her health problems. She joked that it had been suggested to her to use coffee as an enema. Of course, she meant at body temperature, but my immediate thought was, "Hot coffee enemas! What a great idea for my dominant calls!" And I started using it. My callers love it.

I've come a long way, I realize, from doing my first dominant call. I've learned to enjoy being a "Mistress" and to explore a new side of myself. Dominant and submissive are two sides of the same coin. You don't really know the coin until you've turned it over and examined both sides. I value these calls, and I know that I've given something to the caller. I don't delude myself that I have helped him work on his long-term self-esteem problems, but I've given him some much needed attention and a chance to be in control. And I've been there for him, accepting and not judging him.

THE LIGHT OR SENSUOUS DOMINANT CALL

These callers are not really submissive in the same sense as those in the heavy dominant calls. They usually just like to be teased. Sometimes they like to be tied up, which is where the term "dominant" comes from, but a better description for this type of call would be "sensuous directive."

As I have mentioned, this is my favorite type of call. These callers are almost always participatory and often sensuous. They put out a lot of good energy and are appreciative and fun to work with.

One notable characteristic about the sensuous dominant call is that it varies less than any other type of call. The activities are not only standard, they are predictable. The length of the call is almost always about ten to twelve minutes. The energy level starts out high, builds to a climax, and ends high.

I start out by undressing in front of the caller. I describe my outfit—usually either a tight-fitting miniskirt with a low-cut, bright-colored blouse, black lace underwear, and black fishnet hose with high heels, or a tight-fitting body suit. I undress slowly, showing off each part of my body and telling him how wonderful it is, letting him watch but not touch me, no matter how much he begs (and he does).

"See how round and firm my tits are?"
"Oooh, yes! They're wonderful!"
"See how hard my nipples are?"
"Oh, God! Can I suck on them, please?!"
"No, not yet. Just look at how beautiful they are. Think about how good they would taste!"
(Moans.) "I want them so bad!"

Finally I finish undressing, then come up close to him, giving him a better look. I let him touch me, but not as much as he would like. Often, at this point, I tie him down to the bed, then stand or kneel over him and tease him some more. Or I may bite his nipples or his cock (not hard enough to cause any real pain), or fondle or suck his cock, pointing out to him that he can't move or prevent me from doing anything I want to do to him.

I try to elicit as much begging, pleading and body-worshipping I think I can get out of him:

"Tell me how bad you want to put your cock in my pussy."
(Groans). "I'm dying for it! My balls are aching! Please let me have it! Please!!"

Eventually, I permit him to get enough direct stimulation to come. Sometimes I keep him tied down, while I sit on him and ride his cock. Sometimes I make him masturbate while I watch, admonishing him to produce a lot of cum and ejaculate it far, because that's what I like.

I once got a caller who wanted me to be his mother and dominate him sensuously rather than strictly. He wanted me to tease him and order him to perform sexual acts on both me and several of my women friends, while constantly reminding him that I was his mother and it was his obligation to please me.

"Be a good boy, and eat your mommy's pussy."
"I love to eat my mommy's pussy! I love to please my mommy!"
"You're such a good boy! You make your mommy so happy!"
"I love to make my mommy happy!"

He wanted to end by masturbating until he came, while all of us watched him and told him how much we enjoyed watching him get off. I felt that he was one of the most honest callers I had ever had.

Occasionally, I will get a call that mixes strict and sensuous dominant. The caller will want to be abused, but not too severely, and will also want to be teased. Calls like this make me realize that the line between strict and sensuous dominant is a fine one and that the basic scenario is the same: the caller wants a lot of stimulation and attention, but definitely wants to be directed, to be told what to do. Sensuous dominant calls are wonderfully enjoyable, and they energize me for the rest of the evening. Although they don't vary much in content or energy level, they are never boring.

CROSS DRESSERS

Cross dressers are heterosexual males who identify with their feminine side to the point where they like to fantasize about being female. Many cross dressers like to reverse roles: I strap on a dildo and fuck them. There is a whole sub-culture for these guys. They refer to themselves as "sissy boys."

Cross dressers are the easiest callers to work with. Like the callers in the sensuous dominant calls, cross dressers are almost invariably participatory callers, sometimes even sensuous ones. They understand fantasy—they do it all the time.

One of my earliest cross-dresser experiences was with an older caller, perhaps in his sixties. He had three panties that he kept switching among: white lace with roses on them, blue with white lace trim, and black. He associated these with three different roles. When he wore the white ones, he was a sweet little girl; when he wore the blue ones, he was a sensuous woman; when he wore the black ones, he was a "little slut." He would tell me which panties he was putting on, and then I was to call him the appropriate names: "You sweet little girl!" "You sexy lady!" "You're such a little slut!"

What blew me away was that he would intersperse the conversation with, "We girls have to stick together, don't we?" "Yes, we do," I would respond. "We're just alike. We both have pussies," etc. This caller never did get off, though. I felt he had some heavy-duty stuff going on.

Sometimes the cross dresser will give me the power of making him female:

"Give me a pussy and breasts."
"Your tits are so soft! I love to play with them! Spread your legs open so I can see your hot pussy!"

Whether he gives me this power or not, he may want to be fucked as though he were female. He may want to be in a subservient position, such as lying on his back with his legs in the air. I fuck him with a dildo, telling him how deep I am getting into his pussy, how good it feels to him.

Some cross dressers, in fact, like women so much that they want to be lesbians. I once did a call with a guy who wanted me to be his girlfriend and to call him by name: Heather. He wanted us to make love, not just fuck, to be told over and over, "I love you, Heather. I love you so much ..." etc.

This was a strange call, very poignant. It verged on being a pseudo-intimate call, yet it didn't aggravate me the way pseudo-intimate calls usually do. I felt that he knew that this was a fantasy, and that made it okay for me. Also, as with the sensuous dominant caller who wanted me to be his mommy, I felt that this caller was direct and honest. He asked for what he wanted rather than trying to manipulate it out of me.

Some cross dressers want to be sexually abused and humiliated. These are dominant calls, where I take the caller to a party or other public place and he is humiliated by multiple perpetrators. I had one caller who wanted to be dressed up in a frilly little-girl dress, taken to his (her?) own birthday party and abused. I felt that this fantasy had some basis in reality, and felt an overwhelming compassion and poignancy about this call. It was a hard one to let go of.

It amazes me that these female-identifying guys can pretend they have female genitals at the very moment when they are masturbating, holding their hard cocks in their hands. They could hardly pick a time when they should be more aware of their maleness. I never cease to marvel at the power of fantasy.

Not all cross dressers actually want to be female, however. Many of them just want to put on women's underwear. To these callers, I say things like, "Feel how soft and silky those panties feel against your cock! Doesn't that make you so hot you can't stand it?" With this kind of stimulation they usually come pretty quickly.

Cross dressers are generally quick and easy. They are really into fantasy and just need someone to enhance the intensity. They are usually a real pleasure to work with—direct, honest and appreciative.

THE STORY FANTASY

My favorite line to hear from a caller is "I have this fantasy...". "Aha!" I rejoice (silently). "A story! A chance to really act!"

Sometimes when I got the order for a call I would get a clue that it might be a story fantasy. The office would tell me something like, "This guy wants you to be his young cousin." Often, though, I didn't find out until I asked him if there was anything particular he wanted to do, and he would say those magic words. At that point, he would sketch out the story line. Then either he or I would suggest a starting point and describe the physical scene, and we would proceed to carry on a dialogue, to act out a short skit.

A story fantasy can actually be almost any type of call—hot and sexy, bisexual, dominant, submissive. The callers, though, are high-energy—participatory or sensuous. Consequently, these calls, although they require some energy and concentration on my part, are rewarding.

A common theme for story fantasies is an office seduction. The caller wants me to be a woman he works with, that he has the hots for. I might suggest that we start with my coming into his office during lunch hour, when the office is fairly deserted.

"Hi, Bob. Here's the final copy of my section of the report. Do you want to get together and go over it soon?"
"Sure. How about now?"
"OK. Should I close the door?"
"Yes, why don't you?"
"OK."
"You look really nice in that sweater, Jean."
"Why, thank you!"
"It shows off your tits really nice."
"You like my tits, huh?"
"I sure do."
"Would you like to feel them up?"

And so the call progresses from there. After this, it's pretty standard hot-and-sexy stuff, with perhaps a few references to the fact that we had better not get caught. Many story fantasies, in fact, have some added element like this—danger, power or performance issues—which adds another dimension to the call. The caller is not just getting off; he's trying to deal with some other issue as well. He may not be consciously aware of this issue; in fact, the call may be a way of not dealing with it. But he is, at least, in touch with these non-sexual needs enough to have figured out a way of acting them out in fantasy.

This added dimension is what I love about the story fantasy. I am intrigued by the kinds of issues that I see portrayed in the stories.

A lot of non-story calls, of course, have a progression of action that could be called a story. The calls that I refer to as story fantasies, however, start with a lead-in—a non-sexual social theme—then progress into sexual activities. Non-story calls start out being sexual, even though they may have a sequence of events and actions.

Although many story calls are unique, there are also a few standard story fantasies that I hear pretty often. The office fantasy which I described above is one of the most common. Other favorites are the elevator fantasy (I am alone with the caller in an elevator and we get it on), the teacher-schoolboy fantasy (I, the teacher, seduce the caller, an innocent schoolboy), and the medical fantasy (I am a nurse or doctor and seduce my patient). When there is a power difference, as in the teacher and doctor fantasies, there is frequently a dominant-submissive overlay to the story. (The teacher fantasy, of course, is an example of child molestation, which is a special type of story fantasy.)

One of the first story calls I did was with a sensuous southern gentleman who wanted me to be his teenage virgin cousin. He wanted to seduce her, introduce her to sex. One of the key elements in this fantasy, as with many fantasies, was the "forbidden fruit" theme. Several times during the call, he admonished me not to make too much noise because we mustn't get caught. "We're not supposed to be doing this, are we?" "We don't want anyone to know."

Another element in this call, of course, was the virgin seduction, another common theme. Actually, there are two versions of the virgin seduction theme—a sensuous one and a submissive one. The sensuous version plays on the myth of unleashed passion, a passion which has been kept bottled up so long that when it is finally let out it is overwhelming. The submissive version is a brutal rape, an attack on what is perceived as an arrogant aloofness. In this version, the virgin is not only corrupted by the rape but is also exposed for what she "really" is—a slut, hiding behind a facade of purity. This type of virgin seduction call is not usually a story fantasy, however; it is just a standard submissive call.

The southern gentleman's call was the sensuous virgin seduction theme. As I played the hesitant but curious teenager, the caller led me on, tenderly but seductively. He helped me undress, exclaimed over my nubile body ("My, you do have quite a bush, don't you?!" "Those tits are so nice and firm, Honey!"), and was solicitous of my welfare ("I'll put it in slowly so I don't hurt you, Honey."). I alternated between being scared and shy, and passionate ("Will it hurt?" "Is it okay to touch you there?" "Oh! That feels GOOD! I didn't know it could feel like this!"). Until that time, I had never had so much attention and energy directed at me during a call. This was one of those calls that left me feeling high for several days afterward.

I felt particularly good about this call because it seemed to be a way of avoiding incestuous abuse. This caller seemed to have a healthy attitude about his desire for this cousin, who I sincerely believe was a real person. He realized that his desire was natural and healthy, yet he was also aware that it would be inappropriate to act on it. Fantasizing about it was the perfect solution. He got his emotional needs met without exploiting anyone.

I could feel his tenderness and caring, his lust and his sensuality. He had his story worked out in detail—what he wanted to do when—and he led me on a fantastic journey. I felt that I was along for a wonderful joy ride, and all I had to do was be a good actress and respond to his cues.

There is also the flip side of the virgin seduction fantasy, where I am the seducer and the caller is the virgin. Although this is usually an incest/child molestation type of call, I do occasionally get a virgin seduction with an "innocent adult" theme. The one I remember best was a caller who did a really good job of sounding and acting virginal. He wanted me to pick him up in a bar and take him home and seduce him—not a very original theme, but as usual it was the energy he put into the story that made it come alive.

What was most memorable about this call was that the guy's voice and manner of talking reminded me of Benny on L.A. Law. He really sounded innocent and sweet. He knew nothing and wanted me to tell him what to do, how he could turn me on, etc. ("The guys in the office say that I should eat your pussy. But I don't know how to do that. Can you show me?" "Sure, honey. I'll tell you just what to do.") I had to be assertive with him but not aggressive. He wanted a gentle touch, not a hard-nosed hooker approach.

I knew that he was not really a virgin because he asked too many of the right questions. But he was an excellent actor—he played it as well as I did. And it was a wonderful game, one of those calls that made me energized for days afterward. And for a long time after that, I remembered him and smiled whenever I saw Benny on L. A. Law.

I once did a story fantasy with a man who wanted me to do a lesbian seduction of a woman who had spurned him. He had tried to pick her up at a bar where they were dancing together. I created a story line out of this. I was at the bar, dancing with them. I described the way the woman was dressed—in a skin-tight red leather mini-dress, black see-through hose and high heels. I talked about how luscious she looked, how her tits bounced as she danced, etc. Then she and I took a break and went to the ladies' room together. The place was empty. She went into one of the stalls, and I followed her in and closed the door.

I pushed her against the wall and started fondling her breasts. I kissed her. She struggled at first, then started to relax. I unbuttoned her dress and sucked on her tits. I put my hand up her dress and fondled her crotch, pulled her panties aside and felt up her pussy. She was really wet! I pushed her dress up, pulled down her panties and started eating her. She came, her pussy dripping wet on my face.

The caller came, too.

Once, after the brief introductions at the beginning of the call, the caller said that my voice reminded him of a teacher he had had. I asked if he'd had the hots for her. He said yes. I suggested that we play out a fantasy where he was a boy again and I was his teacher and seduced him. This started out in the usual way. I told him that he needed to stay after school, took him into my office, and initiated the standard conversation:

"You sure are getting to be a big, handsome boy, Bobby."
"Gee, thanks, Miss Jones."
"Do you think I'm pretty, Bobby?"
"I sure do, Miss Jones."
"Do you like my tits?"
"Oh, yes, Miss Jones!"
"Would you like to get a better look at them?"
"Oh, yes!"
"I'm going to take off my blouse and bra. Would you like to suck on my tits, Bobby?"

This scenario progressed until I was completely nude. Then, in a abrupt switch, he ordered me to bend over the desk while he whipped me with a ruler. It was a switch-over call! I was caught by surprise but quickly recovered and played along with it. I had done the teacher seduction fantasy several times but never with this development. I wondered later whether it would have been a switch-over call anyway, even if I had not suggested the story. I suspect that it would have.

Sometimes I will get a story fantasy that is difficult for me. One caller wanted to replay an incident that had happened at a fraternity party in college. After most of the girls had left, several stayed behind. These girls had been picked by some of the fraternity leaders for their sexual prowess. The leaders and the girls forced all of the boys to get undressed and perform sexually with them. They made fun of the less well endowed ones, or those who couldn't get it up, while glorifying the ones with bigger cocks and more virility. In this story, I was to be the ringleader of the girls. The caller, of course, was one of the successful ones (at least in the fantasy).

I did this call, but I didn't like it. I considered refusing, but was too intrigued: I wanted to figure out what was going on for this caller.

He obviously had some insecurities about his sexual prowess, and he needed me to validate his virility. In spite of the exploitative nature of the story, he was not an obnoxious, demanding caller. I found it hard to condemn him, felt some compassion, some curiosity, some gratification that I had given him something he needed. Perhaps this fantasy kept him from some harmful acting out.

One of the more bizarre stories that I played out was a call where the customer wanted me to be chased by a giant, who caught me, picked me up in his hands and carried me off, then got out a tape measure and took my measurements. This was one of those calls where I had a hard time suppressing my laughter. I also had a hard time acting this part, although the caller said that I did a good job and he got off okay. ("This giant is chasing me! I'm so scared! I'm running as fast as I can, but I can't get away! I can feel his hands surrounding me!" etc.)

The strangest story fantasy I ever did was one that seemed to be totally non-sexual. The caller wanted me to go over to a girlfriend's house, where I discovered that she was really strung out on drugs. I then called him, told him how worried I was about the girl, and begged him to come over and help me take care of her. ("Please come over and help us, Tom! I'm so scared! We need your help!")

I guess this was the "helpless-females, knight in shining armor" syndrome. I thought that maybe it was a re-enactment of a real situation, but I never was sure that I had it figured out. Whatever it was about, he got off on it.

More than any other type of calls, story calls require my best acting skills. I sometimes have to play a character that doesn't fit me at all. Although this kind of switch can happen in other types of calls as well, it is more difficult in the story call because there I have to converse with people and describe activities that feel foreign to me. I really have to get into the character. I often feel shaky about this, and thank God for the shield that the telephone provides. Yet I feel a real sense of accomplishment when I've done the call successfully.

Story calls are often an adventure, sometimes bizarre, always a challenge to my acting ability. I come away from them feeling that I have gone on a trip to a sort of Alice-in-Wonderland place. Because I've had a glimpse into the caller's perceptions of people and situations, I often feel closer to him than I do to some of the more standard callers. He has taken me on a journey into his internal world.

5

Some Common Variations

In addition to the standard types of calls, there are some themes and variations that I run into fairly frequently. Some of these are just additional activities that are popular, like golden showers; others are particular types of story fantasy calls, like incest. Although many calls include more than one of these variations, I'll talk about each of them separately.

GOLDEN SHOWERS

A lot of people like the idea of being peed on, at least in fantasy. I was surprised to find out how common this was. Not too uncommon also is being shit on or forced to eat shit. Although I use both these activities frequently in my dominant calls, I get a fair number of requests for golden showers even in the "regular" hot-and-sexy calls.

This activity can go in either direction—me peeing on them or them peeing on me—and often it's mutual. When I pee on them, it's a dominant call, for that portion of the call; when they pee on me, I become a submissive for a time.

In case you wonder how you can pee on someone on the phone, here's a sample:

"Anything particular you'd like to do?"
"Yes. I'd like you to pee on me."
"Okay. Would you like to be tied up while I do that?"
"Sure."
"Okay. Lie down on the bed. I'm going to tie down your hands, then spread your legs apart and tie down your feet. You can't move now, can you?"
"No, Mistress."

"I'm going to kneel over your face with my legs apart and pee right in your face. Can you feel that warm pee on your face?"
"Oh, yes, Mistress."
"I'm going to pee in your mouth now. Can you taste that?"
"Yes, Mistress. It tastes good!"
"I want you to swallow it all."
"Yes, Mistress, I will."

If they're peeing on me, it might go like this:

"I'm lying down now. Please pee on my face, in my mouth."
"Okay, here it comes."
"Mmmm. Your pee tastes good!"
"I'm going to pee on your pussy now."
"Oh, please do! Open my pussy lips and pee on my clit! That warm pee feels so good on my clit!"

There are also people who like the idea of watching or listening to someone pee. I had a regular customer like this for quite a while, although he eventually stopped calling. (Perhaps he got as tired of me as I did of him.) He said that he was intrigued by peeing because of an incident from childhood, when he and a little girl took turns peeing in front of each other. They had been caught and reprimanded for this, and he consequently developed a compulsive interest in the topic.

This guy wanted me to take the phone into the bathroom and pee, holding the phone down in the toilet so he could hear it. I didn't actually do this, of course, but figured out a good substitute that provided the proper sound effect. He never knew the difference.

I guess there is something intriguing about urination simply because we use more or less the same organs for doing it as we do for sex. Golden showers is basically an S/M activity in a mild form, so it has the same dynamics as any other S/M activity—dominance and submission, control and manipulation.

A little further out in the realm of sexual activities is an interest in shit. Personally, I have never found shit to be at all erotic, but there are certainly a lot of people who do. It strikes me as being a moderately heavy S/M activity. This perception is borne out by experience: a caller who gets into shit usually gets into other S/M stuff, too.

Occasionally, though, I'll get a standard hot-and-sexy call where the caller will be fucking me in the ass and he suddenly gets into shit—literally:

"Fuck my ass deep with your hard cock!"
"Ooh! I can feel some warm shit up there!"
"Yes! Feel that shit on your cock! Pull your cock out and let me shit on it! Smear my shit all over your cock!"
"Yes, I love to feel your shit all over my cock!"
This can sometimes go on until he comes.

Although I can't say that I feel totally comfortable doing shit calls, I have gotten used to them. Now they seem no more bizarre to me than any other S/M activity. While it's not a sexual activity I relate to, I don't try to analyze it.

INCEST AND CHILD MOLESTATION

I do a fair number of these calls, although they are certainly not what I'd call common. Most of the requests are for mother-son incest, although I get a few father-daughter or brother-sister ones and some out-of-family child molestations, both ways (I am the victim, or the caller is the victim).

Since I have worked with support groups for adult survivors of child sexual abuse for some years, I understand a lot about the dynamics of child molestation. Consequently, I am really good at doing these calls, although I would never condone the acting out. Under no circumstances is child molestation or seduction ever appropriate.

Although I'm not really comfortable being a perpetrator, I do it. This is another case of my being driven by my curiosity. I figure I might learn something.

In a mother-son incest call, I seduce my son (the caller). Usually, it starts out with his coming into my bedroom, either accidentally or at my beckoning, while I am naked in bed and perhaps masturbating. I entice him to stay, telling him that it's time he learned about sex. He'll enjoy it, I tell him, and he'll be pleasing me. Surely he wants to please his mother, doesn't he?

I lead him through all the motions, telling him what to do for me, and stimulating him in turn. Sometimes he is eager, sometimes shy. I adjust my style to suit what he wants. If he is reluctant, I may get angry and order him to cooperate. Sometimes there are dominant elements in the call—I may have to spank him, for instance, or at least threaten to.

I introduce him to all sorts of sexual games, usually ending with intercourse, and we both come. I tell him that he's been a good boy and that we'll do more of this later.

I had a regular customer who had a variation on the mother-son incest call. He claimed that he had actually come close to having intercourse with his mother—they had mutually masturbated each other, and that he was hoping they would actually go all the way eventually. He was living with her, and would claim that he was masturbating with his bedroom door open in hopes that she would see him and come and join in.

This caller made me extremely uncomfortable. I thought he was really sick. But by the time I had done the second call with him, I was pretty sure that his claims were pure fantasy. If they weren't, it was such a sick situation that I couldn't do anything about it, and maybe his fantasies were keeping it under control.

I have done only two father-daughter incest calls. One of them I loved, the other one I hated. Although the topic was the same, the calls were completely different.

The first one was a fantasy about a teenage daughter who accidentally came into her father's bedroom at night when he was masturbating. He didn't see her, and she sneaked out again, but the next morning at breakfast she confronted him. She had lots of questions about what he had been doing. She was frightened and curious at the same time.

I played the innocent, devoted daughter, he the understanding father, educating his daughter about male sexuality.

"Daddy?"
"Yes, sweetheart?"
"What where you doing last night?"
"What did you see, honey?"
"Well..."
"It's all right, honey. You can ask me anything you want."
"Anything?"
"Yes, honey. Now—what did you see that you didn't understand?"
"Well, Daddy, your ... penis ... it was sticking up ... I've never seen it like that. Was something wrong with it?"
"No, sweetheart. It gets that way when I feel really good."
"Really?"
"Yes."
"But ... what makes it happen?"

As this call progressed, I could clearly see the power dynamic unfolding. The father had all of this information that the daughter wanted. He also had her daughterly devotion; she believed everything he said. He talked down to her, condescendingly. But the real kicker came when the show-and-tell portion of the call began, when the father got a hard-on and instructed his daughter on how to fondle him, suck him, etc. The critical line here was, "You know, it's you that's making this happen to me, that's making my penis hard, honey."

"Yes," I thought, "that's the payoff." The sexually abused child is offered this power as compensation for sacrificing her boundaries, her sense of self. Power is a substitute for love. And on some level, every perpetrator is aware of this dynamic.
This call ended with the daughter masturbating her father until he ejaculated into her face. So she didn't even get any sexual satisfaction from the encounter.

I got a lot of compliments on this call: "You played that beautifully! You must be an actress!" I didn't bother telling him how I knew so much.

I got high off this call, even though I thought the behavior was totally inappropriate and immoral. I loved the acting, I loved being good at acting, I loved the compliments. I felt that this caller was fantasizing as a substitute for acting out, and was glad that I could be there to facilitate this process for him. I wondered, however, about his need for power over someone as vulnerable as his daughter. I don't think he was aware how inappropriate that need was.

The second father-daughter incest call I did was with a guy who wanted to reminisce about the incestuous relationship he had had with his teenage daughter. He even called me by a name he chose, not the phone name I use:

"Remember the first time we made it together, Jennifer? It was when you were in eighth grade, when you came home from the football game, and Mom was out of town that weekend."

"Yes, Dad. I came home and you were all alone there."
"Yes, and you came and sat in my lap, and we started kissing."
"It felt good."
"I know it did. It felt good to me, too. Then it wasn't too long before we ended up in bed, didn't we?"
"I remember."
"Then, after that, every Saturday when Mom went to work, you'd come and get in bed with me. You'd beg me to make love to you."
"Yes, I loved to be in bed with you, Daddy."

All during this call I debated about whether I should refuse to continue it. But as usual I was curious. I also don't like to turn away from anything: running away from things I find distasteful seems cowardly to me. I feel that I need to face and acknowledge everything that exists—the farthest reaches of human behavior—if I am going to figure out what life and people are all about. That's why I do phone sex, really.

So I finished this call. Talking with him afterwards, I tried to find out whether the call had any basis in reality. He claimed, however, that he didn't even have a daughter.

I didn't believe him.

He did say, after the action was done, "You must think I'm really sick."
"Oh, no," I replied. "People have all kinds of fantasies; it doesn't mean they're sick."
"Actually," I thought to myself, "I think you're a total jerk."

If I could have gotten any proof that he had really molested his daughter, I would have turned him in. But he wasn't about to confess.

I've had a few brother-sister incest calls, but they have all been submissive calls—an angry brother abusing his sister. These haven't been particularly interesting.

Aside from the incest calls, I also get a few calls about child molestation by non-family members. Although these make me uncomfortable, I do them anyway. I'm always curious to see where the call goes.

These calls are usually, but not always, story fantasies. I did get one call from what sounded like the stereotypical dirty old man who wanted me to be an innocent little girl and just stand in front of him with my dress pulled up while he looked at me and masturbated.

He was insistent that I be totally innocent, that I not use any "dirty words" or do anything seductive. This was a short call.

The usual story, though, is about a little girl, prepubescent or in early puberty, who ventures onto a neighbor's property and finds him masturbating. She might come over for a visit or she might wander into the yard and see him through a window. Curious, she approaches him to get a better look.

He invites her to watch and then to participate. She is shy and self-conscious, perhaps even repulsed or scared (the caller gives me cues about how he wants me to respond). But he leads her on or forces her. These often become submissive calls, where the caller actually tries to hurt the child, to rape her violently, fuck her in the ass, etc.

I also get a few calls, similar to the mother-son incest call, where I am to be an older woman seducing a young boy. Often, the caller will tell me that this is a re-enactment of an incident that really happened, which he may describe in great detail. (If I had any illusions that only men molest children, doing phone sex has shattered them.)

One of the most difficult calls I ever got was from a man who told me about his experiences of abuse in an orphanage where he was left for two years while his parents lived overseas, in the 1940s. A regular practice in the orphanage was administering brutal and painful enemas to the children, as punishment for any rule infraction. This practice was most often visited upon children who had been targeted as trouble-makers. While the caller himself had been a victim of these procedures, the most painful experience for him had been witnessing its performance on an older girl who had been a sort of sister-substitute to him.

I wanted to treat this call like a crisis-line call, but the caller was not ready for that. His final comment on the rape of his friend was, "They did it to her because she was bad." So convinced did he remain of this premise that he still gave himself enemas when he felt he was bad (which I judged to be a good part of the time, considering that he was obviously a survivor of child sexual abuse). He was not ready to acknowledge that he had been unjustly victimized. Neither did he want to play out a fantasy around the incidents; he only wanted to tell me about them. It was hard for me to refrain from telling him that he was a survivor and that there were places he could get help, but he was not ready to hear these things and I had to let go of my expectations for him. I talked to him a couple of other times but on those occasions he just wanted to talk about his relationship problems and made only indirect references to his early experiences. I wasn't sure if he remembered the earlier call, or that I was the one he had talked to. I didn't push him.

Aside from this caller, all of the child molestation and incest calls have been from people who wanted to play out an abuse scenario, either as perpetrators or as victims. In general, these calls make me uncomfortable. I do them partly out of curiosity and partly because I know that I'm one of the best performers around. I figure that if I can do the call effectively, perhaps it will keep the caller from acting out the fantasy. Or, if the caller is the victim of the molestation, maybe the call will help him get in touch with his victimization and empower him to deal with it, eventually.

ETHNIC AND AGE STEREOTYPES

"African-American women are more sensuous."
"All African-American men have huge cocks."
"Asian women are sweet, innocent and submissive."
"Older women are more passionate."
"Young women are hot—can't get enough of it."

Probably my most common request for a specific type of role is for an African-American man as an additional fantasy participant. Usually, this is in the dominant calls from men who want to be abused, but I sometimes get callers who want to watch me get fucked by an African-American man. Occasionally, I'll even get a combination of both.

I remember one night when I got a whole series of weird calls, one of them a story fantasy where the caller wanted me to go with him to a bar and help him pick up an African-American man, whom we took home to fuck both of us.

First, I was to be "it." This black man's cock was not only long, it was also thick, and the caller really got into watching the performance:

"Isn't that cock big? Is it splitting your pussy open so much it hurts?"
"It's so big! I can feel it opening my pussy up! Can you see his black cock fucking my hot pink pussy?"
"Is it hurting you?"
"Oh, it hurts so bad!" (sobbing). "I want him to stop!"
"No, he's going to fuck you harder!"
I sobbed more desperately.

After a while of this, the caller wanted to be fucked in the ass by the African-American man, while I sucked the caller's cock until he came.

I've gotten so used to submissive callers who want to be fucked by an African-American man that I usually volunteer this scenario even without being asked. Something that has surprised me, though, is the number of white men with Southern accents who secretly want to be ass-fucked by an African-American man, or to suck his cock. Of course, there is a double interpretation of this fantasy. On the one hand it indicates a fear of black men, on the other a stereotype of them as sexual degenerates—the very stereotype that led to the lynching of many African-American men throughout the South for several generations.

The next most popular request is for a young woman. Since you have to be eighteen to be a phone sex performer, I can't pretend to be younger (except on those calls where it's clearly understood that I'm doing a fantasy role). The callers who want a very young woman usually want me to tell them stories about what kind of sex

I've done (anal, oral, group, whatever). And they invariably want to know how I lost my virginity, with graphic details about how much I enjoyed it.

"Tell me about the first time you did it. How old were you?"
"It was with my boyfriend. I was 15. We were over at his house, and his parents were away on a trip." (A real original line). "We started making out, then got into it pretty heavy. He felt up my pussy—it was really wet by now ..."
(Caller moans.)
"His cock was so hard! It had never gotten that hard before, other times we'd made out. I really wanted him to put it in!"
"Did you beg him for it?"
"I started to, but it didn't take much convincing. He spread my legs open really wide, then shoved his hard cock up my pussy!" (I groan). "God, it felt good! I couldn't believe how good it felt! I needed it so bad!"
"Did it hurt?"
"A little, at first, but I was so hot, it started feeling good pretty quick."
"Are you wet right now?"
"Oh, I'm dripping wet! I get so hot thinking about that time!"

Once I did a young-woman call and forgot that I was supposed to be young. When the caller asked me about losing my virginity, I replied that that had happened a long time ago, when I was in college. Yet he had bought in to my being eighteen so much that he simply thought he had misunderstood: "It was with a guy who was in college?" "Yes, I was dating this guy in college," I covered myself quickly. "My parents didn't like it that I was going with a guy so much older, but I sure learned a lot from him!" I breathed a silent sigh of relief and thanked God people are so good at shutting out what they don't want to hear.

Other common requests are for me to be a particular ethnic or racial type—African-American, Asian, Hispanic, English. I never accepted an English call because I don't trust myself to not break character, but the service did get occasional requests for them.

When I'm African-American, I'm supposed to be excessively sensuous and to talk about how much better I like white men than black men, presumably because of the power difference. This is a little difficult for me because, in fact, I used to prefer African-American men for the same reasons the callers prefer African-American women—sensuality and power. I can empathize with the white men who want to make it with a black woman, but of course I can't say so in the call.

I had a Jewish customer in Chicago who sincerely believed I was an African-American jazz singer who moonlighted as a phone sex performer. One of his fantasies was to be at a party surrounded by beautiful, intelligent and talented white women, none of whom knew how to be properly sexual. Each of them tried in turn to satisfy him, but finally I had to demonstrate. (I only gave him a blow job, but I did it sensuously.)

I once got a call from an African-American man who had insisted on having an African-American performer. All during the call I worried that he would test me by making some cultural reference that I would not know about, and I would be revealed for the fraud I was. He didn't, however, probably because it never occurred to him that he was being lied to, and I breathed a sigh of relief when the call was over.

Another common request is for an Asian woman. Although most of these are pretty standard calls with not much reference to my being Asian, I do get a few callers who have stereotypes about Asian woman. I remember one particularly low-energy caller—the kind who doesn't say anything. Undaunted, I ran through my standard line: "Let me suck your cock. Ooh, that tastes good! You want to feel up my pussy, feel how wet it is?" When I finally paused, he said, "Asian women don't know words like that! I don't believe you're really Chinese!" I told him I could be sweet and innocent, if that's what he wanted, but the spirit of the call had been corrupted.

I'm surprised how many men don't seem to know much about Asian women's physical characteristics. Although the myth about their vaginas being horizontal instead of vertical does seem to have died away, most men don't seem to know that Asian women have very little, or no, pubic hair.

"Tell me about your pussy hair."
"I don't have much."
"You don't? Why not?"
"Asian women don't have pussy hair."
"They don't?" (Pause.) "Well, pretend you do and tell me about it anyway."
Why did he ask for an Asian, I wonder?

I guess I shouldn't be surprised, really. Most people are appallingly ignorant about sex, even about their own bodies, much less those of the opposite sex and a different racial group. But these misconceptions do make it obvious that I'm dealing not with someone who has experience with that group but with someone who has fantasies about it.

Occasionally I'll get a request to be an older woman—fifty or older. Although these are usually child molestation calls, once in a while it will be with someone who just likes older women. I did several calls with a Russian immigrant who wanted a 50-year-old woman because she would be mature enough to be really good in bed. I finally had to give up doing calls with him because he wanted to marry me.

Golden showers, incest and child molestation, and ethnic and age stereotype requests are the most common of the non-standard activities I come across in my calls. Some of these calls are entertaining for me, some are difficult. Yet these unusual activities have broadened my horizons and have sometimes made me examine my own attitudes and feelings.

In order to be effective in doing these calls, I have had to try to see things from the callers' points of view, to share their perceptions for a while. This has been an enriching experience and has caused me to lift some of my judgmentalism. It's hard to look down on someone after you've looked at the world through his eyes.

6

More Unusual Calls

Along with the standard calls and the common variations, I get a few calls with characteristics that place them outside these categories. These calls are not necessarily more bizarre, they are simply less common—I get fewer of them.

These less common types, however, are often some of the more interesting calls. I don't always enjoy doing them, but I am always entertained and enlightened by them.

"TELL ME A STORY"

"This guy wants a swinging housewife," the phone service woman told me when she gave me the order.

"Okay," I thought. "We'll see what he means by that."
"Are you married?" the caller asked me, after we got through the preliminaries.
"Yes," I replied.
"Do you run around on your husband?"
"Oh, all the time. I'd get bored with just him."
"Did you ever get caught?"
"Well, yes. One time I did."
"How did that turn out?"
"Well, my husband came home unexpectedly from a business trip. I was making it with a couple—a man and a woman."
"Ooh! Tell me more!"
"We were having a great time together. I was eating this other woman's pussy, while the guy was fucking me in the ass, when my husband walked in."
"What happened then?"

"Well, he was pretty pissed off. He just couldn't believe I would do such a thing. But, there were three of us, and we started making him do things with us."
"Like what?"
"We took off all his clothes, then we took turns spanking him. He started crying. We told him to shut up. Then the other guy started fucking him in the ass, while the other woman made him eat her pussy. He didn't like it, but he couldn't do anything about it."

This caller wanted me to provide some entertainment for him, so I decided to do it in a big way. I could have gotten away with a simple story about my husband finding me with another man, then felt out what the caller wanted and gone on from there. Often, though, I try to go overboard in these calls: "You want entertainment? I'll give you more than you bargained for."

I enhance these stories partly in hopes of getting the caller off sooner, partly just to see how he'll react, and partly out of resentment at being asked to provide more than my share of the energy in the call. For the "tell me a story" calls differ from the story fantasy calls: here I am the one making up the story, and that takes a lot more energy and concentration than following someone else's story.

Although this particular caller was fairly high energy and told me pretty much what he wanted, the more typical "tell me a story" type is lower-energy and more demanding. He has some hidden agenda which he won't tell me. For example, he may want a racial or age stereotype call. This request will usually come out in the form of a question or comment while I'm in the middle of something else:

"What would you like to do tonight?"
"I want you to be kinky."
"Well, how would you like to stick your hard cock up my tight ass?"
"Sure, that sounds okay."
"Shove it deep up my ass! Split my ass open with that stiff cock!"
"Do you like black men?"
"Oh, yeah! I love to fuck black men!"
"Tell me about a time you let a black man fuck you up the ass."

"Well, I met this guy at a party. I could tell he was real well hung from the bulge in his crotch. So I invited him into a back room ... "
"Did you start out by sucking his cock?"
"Yes. He pulled down his pants and then pushed me down in front of him and shoved his cock in my mouth ... "

As with most demanding callers, it's usually safe to assume that these guys want bizarre stories, with some S/M thrown in for excitement. If I come up with a good enough story, they are usually happy. The main thing I have to watch out for is that if they call again, I don't give them the same story.

Although it's sometimes fun to create bizarre stories, it can also be draining. The demanding callers put me on the spot without giving me any hint of what turns them on, and I resent having these undefined expectations put on me. The higher-energy ones can be more fun, but I need to be awake and alert for these calls.

ANIMALS

Requests to bring animals into the action are usually either dominant or submissive calls, although not always. There are three variations of the animals call—I make it with an animal, the caller makes it with an animal, or I pretend to be an animal. This last type is extremely rare.

I got a request to make it with a dog on my very first night on the phone sex line. Although the service was supposed to be screening out difficult calls for me, they can't be 100% effective because a lot of callers don't ask for what they want until they talk to the performer directly. I did a poor job of this call, not just because of the novelty of it, but also because I hadn't yet figured out how to describe scenarios over the phone.

A couple of days later, I talked to one of my friends who was a sex therapist. He gave me some really helpful feedback. First, he had a really nonjudgmental interpretation of the animal call, saying that some people who grew up on farms find bestiality erotic; it's a natu-

ral outcome of living around animals a lot. This perception was
borne out for me many months later, when I got a call from a
rancher who told me pretty much the same thing.

Secondly, my friend suggested that whenever I was stumped over
how to do a call, I put the burden on the caller, letting them describe
the action: then I could just respond to it. I started doing this, with
all types of calls. It worked out well, and I learned a lot more that
way. (This friend has since died of AIDS. I would have mentioned
his helpfulness at his memorial service if I had had the opportunity
to speak.)

And so I learned to do animals. Like every other type of call, this
wasn't too difficult once I started paying attention to what the caller
wanted and learned a little about bestiality. This is basically a submissive call, and I just have to respond to the caller's abuse. Sometimes, with a low-energy caller, I have to get more active and describe the action. After I talked with the rancher, though, I had a
little more knowledge that I could use to embellish the call. For example, he told me that after a male dog reaches orgasm, the head of
his penis swells up. (I have since had this information confirmed
from other sources.) So I mention this, if I ever need to.

The situation where the caller wants to be raped by animals is easier
for me to do because I can feel more detached from the action. (I
can't say that fucking with animals is really my idea of a good time.)
The only times this request has come up for me, so far, have been
where the caller wants to be raped, either anally or orally or both,
by a male animal, usually a dog. I haven't come across anyone who
wanted to fuck a female animal.

I once did a 20-minute call with a high-energy submissive who told
me, at the beginning of the call, exactly what types of abuse he
wanted: "I want a good 20 minutes of dominance. I want you to
spank me and whip me, fuck me with a dildo. I want to suck off
your man, your dog—whatever you want me to. You can put anything you want up my ass. I want to be your toilet. I want to be
degraded and humiliated in any way you can think of."

"Gee, this sounds like fun," I thought. I proceeded to carry out all of the humiliating and painful things I could think of—whipping, burning, peeing and shitting on him, having my "boyfriend" rape him both anally and orally. Finally, I paused for breath and asked, "Is there anything else you'd like?"

"Yes, I want to suck off your dog," he replied.

"Oh, the dog!" I thought to myself. "How could I have forgotten about the dog?"

So I threw in a horse too, for good measure, partly to make up for my neglect in forgetting the dog. He loved it. "I've never been fucked by a horse before! How big is that horse's dick?" "About three feet long," I replied. (I have no idea if this is an accurate figure or not, but I thought it sounded good. I'll have to check this out with the rancher next time I talk to him.) "Feel it splitting your ass open!" He moaned convincingly.

Once in a great while, I'll get a caller who wants to harass me by demanding that I pretend to be an animal. The first time this happened was a night that I had decided I wanted to take a hot bath and thought I would try doing calls from the bathtub.

What I hadn't taken into account, however, was how water amplifies sound. Usually, when I have to get loud in a call, I put my head under a pillow. I do worry somewhat about my neighbors hearing me: "What *is* she doing over there? And there isn't even an extra car in her carport!"

I was particularly concerned about this situation because I lived at that time in an apartment where my bathtub was against the wall of the adjoining apartment, and my next-door neighbor worked for the same company I did on my regular, daytime job.

So here I was in the bathtub, with a dominant caller demanding that I beg to be fucked.

"I need your cock so bad! My pussy is so hot for it!"

"Bark for it!"

"Do what?"
"Bark for it, you bitch!"
So I did, of course. Screw the neighbors, anyway.
I've had many good laughs over this call, not to mention the cir-
cumstances.

Once I got a really demanding caller who wasn't satisfied with my
just being a dog but wanted me to do a pig, a horse and a cow, too.
This was one of my more challenging calls. Fortunately, I wasn't in
the bathtub this time. (Pig vocalizations, by the way, are particularly appropriate for a submissive; they sound really degrading.)
He never did get off. He was one of those who was so burned out
that he couldn't get any real stimulation anymore.

Animals make an interesting addition to calls. They're not a very
common request item, but they do turn up every once in a while.
Usually when I least expect them.

UNDERWEAR PEOPLE

"My neighbor just left her panties in my mailbox. As soon as I
found them, I ran right into the house and called you."

He had called me before. He was married and was having an affair
with his neighbor. "Are they wet?" I asked him.

"Oh, yes! I can smell her pussy juices on them."

Underwear people were one of the surprises I got when I started
doing phone sex. I hadn't known there were such people. I knew
about cross dressers, but underwear men are not the same. Cross
dressers want to wear women's underwear themselves. Underwear
men want their women to wear it, and then they really get into the
underwear itself, after it has the smell, the aura, of the body that it
was in touch with. Furthermore, underwear men are only interested in panties. I never got one that was into bras or other lingerie,
as the cross dressers are.

Sometimes these guys just want me to wear panties at the beginning of the call to help them get aroused; sometimes they want it through the entire call. And unlike the cross dressers, who usually want me to describe the panties in detail, underwear men are more into the fact that the panties smell of my pussy or are still warm from my body. They may want to lick the panties while I'm still wearing them, or to rub their cock against them, or even to take the panties off me and masturbate with them. A lot of them can get off just on this stuff; they don't need to go on and fuck me or get a blow job or anything else.

These were difficult calls for me at first. I'm not much into women's underwear myself; most of it is impractical and even uncomfortable, more of an inconvenience than anything else. I couldn't understand how it could be appealing to someone. Although I like and admire women's bodies, I couldn't relate to women's underwear.

Nevertheless, I learned to do these calls. I listened to the callers to figure out what it was they liked and to talk about it. Generally, they like soft, silky panties, skimpy enough to show some pubic hair, but not too revealing. With these guys, crotchless panties are out: there has to be the enticement of hidden pleasures.

"What kind of panties are you wearing?"
"They're red lace, string bikinis, real see-through. Can you see my pussy hair through them?"
"Oh, yes!"
"I'm spreading my legs open. Can you see how wet the panties are from my pussy juices?"
"Yes, I can. Is your pussy really hot?"
(Moaning) "Oh, it's so hot! Won't you feel it, through my panties?"
"I want to put my cock up against your panties."
"Yes, rub your cock against those soft, silky panties. Feel how smooth they are against your cock?"
(Caller moans.)

For a long time, I wondered what the draw was in used underwear. I think it's just the sense we have that the essence of a person's body lingers in their garments. If we can feel this in a non-sexual sense (hugging an absent loved one's old sweater to us), why not do it with sexual feelings as well? Besides, there's no risk involved, no complications of dealing with a real human being. This could be a big draw for someone who has trouble being in real relationships.

SHE-MALE

Before I started doing phone sex, I had never heard of a she-male. This was part of the education in sex that my being a performer has provided.

A she-male, for those who don't know, is a mythical creature with a mostly female body, but male genitals and male physical strength. She (he?) has all of the appearance of being female --body fat, lack of body hair, soft skin, breasts—but her genitals are male. I suppose there may be some real-life inter-sexed persons who have some of these qualities, but I don't think that any person exists who has a fully developed female body with fully developed male genitals.

There are men who go part way through sex change operations—while they have breasts and may be taking female hormones, they still have male genitals. But they don't really have the body fat, soft skin and female voice that a true she-male is supposed to have. We had one of these people working for the service at one time, but we had to let him go because callers complained that he sounded like a man, which of course he was.

Usually, a caller who requests a she-male is intrigued by male genitals. He wants to know how big my cock is, what it looks like, what I like to do with it. He may want to suck on it or feel it up his ass. Or he may just want to hear details of how I have fucked unsuspecting men that I have picked up.

I tell tales of going into bars, acting seductive and feminine, then taking my prey home and tying him up and fucking him till he begs for mercy. To make this scenario properly juicy, I usually make the man in the story a respectable middle-aged businessman. These calls give me a way to fantasize revenge on some of the jerks I used to have to deal with at work when I was younger and not as empowered as I am now.

I did one call where the caller wanted me to fantasize a third-party she-male, rather than being one myself, and to order him to suck her off. This call really seemed weird to me because of using language like "her dick." It was okay to fantasize that I had a cock, but to use the feminine pronoun in conjunction with male body parts was difficult.

One time I got a caller who believed in the myth that I was a real she-male and wanted to meet me and marry me. He was retiring from the military, he explained, and wanted to settle down now with a nice she-male. "I want a nice-looking woman that I can take out to dinner, take out socializing, then I want to go home and suck your cock," he explained in all seriousness.

He elaborated at length on his secure financial situation, his respectability, his amicable personality. How could I refuse such a offer? What she-male wouldn't jump at the chance?

I tried to explain that I wasn't interested in getting married, but this didn't seem to register. I tried to focus the call on here and now —"What can I do to get you off?" He did manage to come, but then he started in on his spiel again. Finally I told him that I would speak to some of my she-male friends to see if one of them would be interested. I didn't have the heart to tell him that the myth wasn't real, and besides, he might have called the office back and complained that he had been cheated on the call. I was relieved that he was on the other side of the country.

This call made me sad. I felt that he was really gay, but didn't want to deal with the real-life issues around that.

I consider she-male calls to be one of the weirder types that I do. I assume that the caller usually knows that it's a fantasy, but I do wonder what drives it. This is not something that I try to analyze, however.

FOOT FETISHISTS

I have done very few of these calls, and I can't say that it's something I really get into. These guys want me to describe my feet, making them sound really sensuous and sexual. This is somewhat of a challenge, since I don't have a clear idea of what makes feet sexual. I must do okay, however; I've never had a complaint.

Some of these guys go all the way with my feet, putting their cock between them and masturbating themselves that way. (You've heard of tit-fucking; this is foot-fucking.) Others, like some of the underwear people, just need the foot stuff to get aroused, then go into a normal call.

"My feet are narrow and delicate, size six and half double-A shoe size." (This is one part of my body I don't lie about.) "Do you like my feet?"
"Oh, they're beautiful! Can I suck on your toes?"
"Sure, though you'll tickle me." (I laugh.)
"Can I put my cock between your feet?"
"Oh, please do! Feel my feet around your cock! Fuck my feet!"
"Oh, God! It feels so good!"
"Would you like to put your cock between my tits?"
"No, I just love your feet!"
Another challenge...

OVERLY ENDOWED

For a while, I was getting quite a rash of callers who claimed to have over-sized cocks—12, 14, 16 inches long. They didn't seem to want to fuck, though; they mostly just wanted to tell me about the problems they had finding women big enough to accommodate them. They'd ask me if I was big enough: "Sure, honey, you can fuck me, I can take it," I'd tell them.

I have since been told by one of my straight men friends that there is a correlation between the size of a woman's mouth and the size of her vagina. Evidently, women with big mouths like Carol Channing have large-capacity vaginas; women with smaller mouths have a smaller capacity. Unfortunately, though, I haven't had any more of these callers since I got this information.

One of these callers asked specifically for a Hispanic woman because he thought she would be big enough to take his cock. (Makes a big difference over the phone.)

"Are you a big girl? How big is your pussy?"
"How big is your cock?"
"Sixteen and a half inches."
"Ooh, that's big! Can I suck on it?"
"Can you take that much in your mouth?"
"Sure, some of it, anyway. Shove it into my mouth, let me suck it."
"Can you take it in your pussy?"
"Oh, I want it! I want to feel it so deep inside me!"
"Are you sure you can take it? I haven't found a woman who can take it yet. They're scared of it."
"I love big cocks! My pussy is plenty big enough for them."
"I don't know what to do. I go to bars and pick up big, tall women, but when we get home and they see my cock, they won't let me put it in."
"Well, you can put it in me, honey."
"What do you think I should do? What kind of woman should I look for?"
"Have you thought about trying out for porno movies? I bet you could get a job."

I have already mentioned my regular caller who was not well-endowed himself but who was obsessed with big cocks on other men. He's the only one of these I've ever had, except for those callers who are intrigued by the stereotype of the overly endowed African-American man.

VOYEURS AND EXHIBITIONISTS

Occasionally, I'll get someone who wants to either confess to me or do a story fantasy about some aberrant sexual behavior, such as voyeurism or exhibitionism. One caller confessed that he was in the habit of driving down the freeway, following women in other cars, masturbating and getting off. I asked him if he ever lost control while driving when he came, but he claimed he didn't.

Another caller I talked to was an exhibitionist who wanted to sit in his car, parked on the street, and masturbate while I watched. I was supposed to want desperately to fuck with him and beg him to let me in the car to fondle or suck his cock, but he would only tantalize me.

I wasn't sure if this was an activity which he was in the habit of performing or only a fantasy. I'm sure that the part about a woman watching him and wanting him was fantasy, but I'm not sure about the sitting in the car masturbating part.

I've also done several voyeurism story fantasies. For example, I might be riding a bus or subway, wearing a revealing blouse and a miniskirt, sitting across from the caller, trying to tantalize him.

"I'm sitting across from you, wearing a real low-cut blouse, so you can see my cleavage. Can you see my tits bouncing while the train runs?"
"Oh, I love to watch your tits bounce!"
"I'm wearing a really short skirt, and when I'm sitting down, it rides up my legs. Can you see my panties? They're black, and you can't tell for sure if it's my pussy hair you're seeing."
"Oh, I want to see some more! Spread your legs apart more!"
Eventually, I would get off the bus, he would follow, and the standard story fantasy would ensue.

I think that voyeurism, and perhaps exhibitionism too, are more common fantasies than people might imagine. Although the activities may be uncommon, the fantasies are probably not.

TECHNICIANS

These are guys who get so hung up on the technical details of sex that they seem to lose track of the purpose—i.e., having fun and getting off. They are high-energy callers in the sense that they talk a lot and take charge of the call, but they feel like low-energy types because they are so draining. They go into minute graphic details of what they are doing to me, or perhaps what they want me to be doing to myself:

"I want you to put your thumb on your clit, your index and middle fingers into your pussy, and spread your pussy lips open with your other two fingers. Then take your other hand and put two fingers up your ass. Now stroke those fingers in and out of your ass while you rotate the fingers in your pussy around and around, and stroke your clit up and down..."

I try to do some moaning and groaning and "Oh, that feels so good!", but they don't even seem to hear me because they're so absorbed in their own performance. They're really a type of demanding caller, not satisfied with anything. I would hate to really be in bed with one of these guys; they're like machines. They're more concerned with their own technical abilities than they are with enjoying themselves.

(In fact, I have come across some technicians in real life, and they're a real drag. They're the result of the "women can enjoy sex, too" movement of the sixties. Many men now measure their worth by a woman's responses. Although this may seem like an improvement over measuring their worth by their stamina or number of sexual partners, it still puts the burden on the woman to reflect the man's prowess. They make me feel like an orgasm-producing machine.)

COUPLES

I've taken calls from only a handful of male-female couples, not enough to make any real generalizations. I've enjoyed most of them because I like having the opportunity to talk to women. But the couples have all been a bit strange.

The first time I did a couple, I wasn't warned ahead of time. The caller referred to his girlfriend's being there, but I thought that this was just his fantasy. It's not uncommon for a caller to claim, obviously falsely (I can tell by his voice), that he has another woman there with him, usually his regular girlfriend. Sometimes she's there from the beginning of the call, sometimes she walks in on us. She's jealous and wants either to get in on the action or to cut me out. Often, the caller and I gang up on her and abuse her.

So when this caller told me that his girlfriend was there, I didn't take him seriously. But more than five minutes into the call, she came on the phone herself. Actually, all she did was moan— I never did get any conversation from her. But I did help her get off—twice. I tried to get her to come a third time, but she just wasn't up for it. This was hard for me to understand, but I guess some women do have a more limited capacity. Or maybe she'd had an overdose earlier in the day.

The next time I did a couple, the phone service told me about it ahead of time. I got the man off, and then the woman wanted me to, as she said, "seduce" her. So I went through a long, sensuous seduction with her, and she came. But she evidently wanted something more; she still kept saying, "Seduce me."

It turned out that what she really wanted was a more brutal assault, to be raped with a dildo. So I ran through this scenario, too. She liked it and came even better than before.

I'm tempted to make a generalization about women not asking for what they want, but I know that one individual is not enough to make generalizations about.

Another couple I did was on the same night that I did the call where both the caller and I got fucked by an African-American man. (As I said, it was a strange night.) This was a married (so they said) couple in Texas. Although they had a 15-minute time limit, I let the call go on for 22 minutes. It was long and frustrating. Mostly, they wanted me to tell them what to do with each other. I thought, "You guys are married and you haven't figured that out yet?"

So I gave the man instructions on what to do for his wife to make her come. After much struggle, she finally came. Then it was his turn. He was a tough one, though; just couldn't get off. All three of us struggled for some time, trying everything in the book. But he was just too burned out. Or maybe he had made it earlier in the day and hadn't recovered. At any rate, he never did get off. I figured, screw it, I got the woman off, that's what counts. I knew I was being a female chauvinist, thinking this way, but it was a good rationalization. The truth is, I was tired and bored with the call.

I've been disappointed in the women callers I've had. I expected them to be more interesting or intelligent than the men, but haven't found this to be true. In fact, the most abusive, invasive caller I ever got was a woman who was part of a married-couple job. It's not that she was a dominant, although there was a part of the call where she wanted to pee in my mouth, and she started calling me "bitch." But most of the time she was just extremely invasive, wanting to know everything about me. This was a call within the same city where I live, and she wanted to know what lesbian bars I went to. (She didn't know about the same ones I did.) What this couple really wanted was for me to come over in person, and they were trying to track me down. It's partly because of situations like this, rare as they are, that I use a false physical description.

I stuck this call out, abusive as it felt, lying right and left. I finally hung up when they went five minutes over their time limit. She was trying to find out what nude beaches I went to.

I did get one woman who called on her own. She said she was straight but just wanted to see what it would be like to be with a woman. This was a delightful call for me. Actually, I would have liked for it to go on longer, but she came only once and didn't want any more.

UNCLASSIFIABLES

A few rare calls don't fall into any identifiable category. This is not because they are any more bizarre, actually; it's just that I get so few of them that I can't really call them a category. If I got more of them, I'd create a category for them.

One type of call that I get from time to time is guys who want to come more than once. These are more annoying than interesting. I usually assume that once I get the guy to come I'm done with the call, but there are those who want to go through the whole thing all over again.

If they were women, this wouldn't be so annoying, because when women have multiple orgasms, they have them pretty close together, one after another. Once a woman reaches orgasm, she stays at a plateau for a while, during which she can move in and out of orgasm. But men have to go through the whole process of arousal and climax again. Not only does this take time, but it is also more difficult on subsequent times around.

The worst thing about these calls is that they are usually from demanding callers, not (as you might expect) from sensuous ones. Occasionally, I'll get a sensuous caller who wants to do multiple orgasms, but they are few and far between. And even these calls I find to be really draining. I remember one that I did with a caller who was almost constantly moaning and groaning during the whole call. He was high energy and enjoyable, but I was getting tired of it all. And since I had forgotten to write down the time the call started, I ended up giving the guy about twice the time he had paid for. Finally, I asked, "What can I do to get you to come?" "Oh, honey!" he exclaimed. "I came four times!"

"Now you tell me," I thought.

Another type of call that I get occasionally is a fascination with pubic hair. Some guys are really into this and want to lick and even suck on my pubic hair. They like me to have a lot of it, thick and coarse. These calls are among my least favorite; I'm somewhat repulsed by body hair myself.

I've also done one or two calls with guys who used Latin words for sexual organs—vagina, penis, labia. I was surprised at how uncomfortable this made me feel. While I have no hesitation at saying "cock" or "dick," it was really hard for me to say "penis." Maybe it felt too real, too invasive. It certainly felt awkward: "Your penis is so hard! I like your penis so much!" It felt, too, as though I were trying to mix science and sensuality.

The most fun call I ever did was with someone who was into tickling. I get off on this, myself—I'm extremely ticklish. I can also laugh hysterically, with no provocation. So we really got into it. He described, in detail, how he was tickling me:

"I'm going to tie you up, so you can't move. Then I'm going to tickle you with a feather. First around your neck and shoulders ... then, under your arms ... along your sides ... " (I was laughing supposedly uncontrollably by this time) "... are you sure there's no one there tickling you?"

(I stopped laughing long enough to answer.) "No, I'm here alone, and I'm not even tickling myself."

This guy was also a foot fetishist, although he didn't want to put his cock between my feet. He just tickled my feet and got into playing with them for a while. Then he wanted me to tickle him, but since he wasn't able to laugh on cue, as I was, it was harder for me to really get into it. Eventually, we made it the regular way. I had a great time with him.

Another request I've gotten a couple of times was to have milk in my breasts. This wasn't hard for me to get into, since I nursed my own son. I knew exactly what it felt like and also what human milk tasted like, since I had sampled some. So I let these guys suck on my tits and told them about the warm, sweet milk that they were getting.

I've had one or two calls from guys who wanted me to be pregnant. I don't know if this is a fascination with fertility or some kind of a power trip—dominating, in effect, two people at the same time. Or perhaps, like the milk-in-tits calls, it's a desire for some mothering. I do know that I was really horny when I was pregnant, and I played this up during these calls.

One time I got a call from a guy who was really obsessed with the fact that he was circumcised. He wanted me to talk about how much better I liked circumcised cocks than uncircumcised ones. (Actually, as much as I like Jewish men, the opposite is true for me.) At first I wasn't sure exactly what he wanted, but it turned out that he thought that circumcised cocks were less sensitive than uncircumcised ones, and that they needed excessive stimulation. What he really wanted was some mild domination—biting his cock, digging my fingernails into it, and finally squeezing it really tight with my pussy, which finally got him off.

One of the most challenging calls I ever got was from a mildly dominant caller who wanted not only to tie me up but also to gag me. Then I was supposed to scream while he fucked me painfully up the ass. Screaming with my mouth closed was a new experience: "Mmmmmm...mmm! mmmph!" and I had to do it loudly enough to impress him. I was successful, however, and then he wanted to change places: I bound and gagged him and fucked him up the ass with a dildo. He was a pretty good actor himself; in fact, I would classify him as a sensuous caller.

One of the strangest calls I ever got was a request to be an amputee. This caller was intrigued by the idea of making it with a woman with no legs. Actually, he seemed to want to talk more than to fuck, although I did get him off. He wanted details about my accident and recovery. I tried to be as realistic as I could. Evidently I was effective, for he finally said, "I didn't think they were really going to give me somebody who'd had their legs amputated, but you sound like you did. Are you for real?"

I told him no, and he explained that when I talked about being in a support group for disabled people, that was when he started to wonder. I had just tried to figure out how it would be and went for it. It worked.

.   .   .   .

I've certainly had a variety of types of calls. I've been amazed to find out how many different ways people can get off—some that I would never have thought of. This aspect of my phone sex experiences has definitely broadened my horizons. In the area of sexual fantasy, there isn't much that can surprise me any more. I'll talk more in the next two chapters about how these experiences have changed my perceptions of other people and of myself.

7

The Power of Sex, the Fantasy of Self Esteem

We human beings seem to have a talent for complicating activities that other animals appear to do simply, directly, and without fanfare. This phenomenon is evident in all of the activities we perform to meet our basic needs—eating, giving birth, defending our territory, protecting ourselves from the elements, playing and most of all sex. Sex is perhaps unique among these activities in that it ties together so many different aspects of life. It connects us to our bodies, to other people, to birth and to death. We are drawn to its excitement, yet we fear the vulnerability it makes us feel. It is, perhaps, the only social activity where we are allowed to be truly uninhibited—in fact, we have to be for it to work.

This freedom from constraint opens the door for all kinds of other feelings to enter in—anger, fear of abandonment or inadequacy or death, needs for attention and approval and nurturing—all of the feelings which civilization so effectively suppresses. And sexual fantasy, even more than real live sex, provides an arena where many of these "unacceptable" feelings can have free rein. In fantasy there is no real interaction with other people. The other participants in the fantasy are idealized figures created by the fantasizer's imagination.

As a phone sex performer, I try to play the parts of these idealized characters as accurately as I can. In order to perform effectively, I have to try to get inside my callers' heads, to see the images they see. This has been a fascinating journey, a continual adventure. From it I have gained a perspective that I don't believe I could have obtained any other way.

What has struck me most of all about my phone sex experiences is the total buy-in my callers seem to have to the idea that sex holds some kind of an answer for their lives. It will provide entertainment if they're bored, relief if they're tense, attention if they're feeling neglected, stimulation if they're numbed out, power if they're feeling helpless. It cures what ails you.

Different types of callers use different methods of getting these needs met. The low-energy callers soak up energy from me, expecting me to fill a vacuum for them. The sensuous callers are into escape and excitement. Sex is like a carnival ride to them—fast-paced, thrilling, stimulating several senses at once, involving their whole body. The angry callers want me as an object on which to vent their rage. The invasive callers need me to validate their sexual feelings—to tell them that it's okay to let go.

Yet no one seems to question the basic premise that sex is the cure-all. No matter what the specific feelings or fantasies, this underlying assumption pervades all types of calls. That's what phone sex is all about, of course. People wouldn't be wanting it and paying for it if they didn't think it would fix something for them.

Being on the outside, though, I have a different perspective. Even while I'm playing roles, I stand aside, watch the action, and analyze everything I can. I'm an analyst by nature.

It is my observation that there are four major dynamics that go on in phone sex fantasies: the desire to be entertained and to escape from reality, obsessive fantasies, power issues and, underlying all of these, the need for attention, affection and validation.

ENTERTAINMENT AND ESCAPE

Most phone sex calls involve, at least to some degree, this desire to be "taken away from it all" to a more exciting place. That's the whole idea of fantasy, after all—escape from reality.

This need is most evident in some of the more intense calls. The demanding caller's constant need for more entertainment, more stimulation, is a cry for rescue from a reality that is too boring, or perhaps too painful, to face. Similarly, both sides of the S and M scenario reflect a need for extraordinary stimulation. And some types of calls have entertainment as their primary theme—story fantasies, she-male calls, voyeurism fantasies.

The ultimate escape artists, though, are the cross dressers—particularly the strongly female-identified ones. They want to deny a basic facet of their identity—their gender. Yet sometimes I think that the cross dressers are more honest about their need for escape than some of the other callers who think that they're being sophisticated with their bizarre fantasies.

Of course, as a performer I get a fair amount of entertainment and escape from phone sex myself. Often, especially during some of the higher-energy calls, I have a vision of myself and the caller as being surrounded by a sort of energy field that we have created together out of our imaginations. We come into this space during the call, carry out our fantasy, then go back to our own separate realities. In spite of this vision, however, I don't think that I get quite the buzz from the fantasy that the caller does. I'm not, after all, getting sexually aroused; I'm getting high off the fun of acting, which is not as intense or as compelling.

Nevertheless I can certainly understand the appeal of sexual fantasy as a method of getting away from the tedium of ordinary reality. And escape isn't necessarily negative, at least not in moderation. Although habitual escape can be destructive, an occasional fling can be fun and exciting. There are many callers who do phone sex only once every two or three months, or even less frequently. For these people, phone sex is probably just one of many outlets for sexual release.

When overindulged in, though, sexual fantasy can be like a drug. The presence of sexual hormones in the bloodstream does in fact have a real physiological effect on the brain similar to an artificial chemical substance. This is a powerful mind-altering substance, even addictive

for some people. But as with any other addiction—drugs, worka-
holism, gambling—sexual fantasy is, I believe, a symptom of some
feeling of emptiness within. "Fill me up with energy, make me come
alive." And like the other addictions, fantasy works, at least until the
user develops a tolerance for it. The glow can last for days afterwards.

OBSESSIONS AND FASCINATIONS

Although the opportunity to escape into a fantasy world is enough for
many people to get off, some callers seem to be drawn to very specific
types of sexual activity or to some particular type of person or part of
the body. Sometimes this interest develops into a full-blown obsession; for other people, it is just a fascination—they are intrigued by a
particular aspect of sexuality.

Fascination with a particular ethnic or age group, or a specific body
type is one form of the obsession or fascination call. These callers
have an idealized version of a certain type of person: "If only I could
be ass-fucked by a really big black cock," "I want a hot young pussy,"
"I need an older woman, with humongous tits."

This is one of the big draws of phone sex, of fantasy in general: perfec-
tion—the perfect partner, the perfect fuck. Although this seems innocent enough, I often wonder what it is about that particular fascination that means so much to the person.

As I have pointed out, the most common fascination, the well-
endowed African-American man, seems to be especially popular
among Southern white men. It makes sense to me, as I believe there is
a real fear among any class of people who oppress others, of those
whom they oppress. (Thomas Jefferson lived in fear and guilt, convinced that someday the African-American people would rise up and
attack their white "owners." He also had an African-American mistress.) To a white man, being raped by a black man may seem just ret-
ribution for the degradation to which whites have subjected African-
Americans.

Less common but along the same lines is the sensuous African-American woman theme. While this scenario differs from the dominant / submissive African-American man theme, it still has elements of fear in it. The myth is that the African-American woman is the ultimate sexual partner—overflowing with sensuality, skilled in sexual technique, joyful in her femininity, appreciative of her male partner and able to make him feel sensuous and uninhibited himself. There is in this picture a certain awe of the sexual powers of the African-American woman, almost a worshipfulness.

In general, I think people of color represent to white people a sort of earthiness and sensuality. Those qualities have great appeal to an overly technologized people who are cut off from their basic needs and feelings. And of course sexuality is perceived as a direct path to that world of sensuality and the emotions. Having sex with an African-American person seems to be a quick ticket to that world. (The negative side of this stereotype, of course, is that it perceives African-Americans as only earthy and sensual—an attitude that fosters oppression.)

Fascinations with other ethnic groups or nationalities, such as Asian, Latin or English, are probably also attempts to escape into other worlds of either sensuality or refinement. The stereotypes of sweet, submissive Asian women, fiery, sensuous Latinas, or refined English ladies with hidden passions are probably at work in these fantasies.

The fascinations with either very young women or older, mature women are also, I believe, attempts to get in touch with sensuality or emotions. In the case of younger women, it is a need to be overwhelmed with youthful energy and sensuality, or to control or overpower someone; in the case of older women, it is a need to be nurtured and appreciated. (I refer here to non-abusive fantasies with older women, not to the child molestation calls.)

Fascination with particular body parts is another intriguing issue. Of course, it's pretty common to be more appreciative of one part of the body over another; most men have their favorite (ass men, leg men, etc.) When this fascination becomes obsessive, though, I wonder if something else may be going on—perhaps a suppressed sexual abuse memory or some unfulfilled need. For example, I have observed in real life that men who were breast-fed as babies are much less interested in breasts than are those who were bottle-fed.

A fascination with oversized cocks is often, I think, an indication that a man may really be gay, although he may not be aware of this himself. Cock size seems to be a much bigger issue for men than it is for women. I hear a lot about it from my gay men friends, whereas women don't care. (Any woman who says she does is most likely lying to please men.) I wonder, therefore, about the callers who are obsessed with big cocks. I would never venture to suggest to them, however, that they might be gay. I don't feel that sure about it, and even if it's true, they're probably not ready to deal with it.

As far as some of the less common obsessions go—foot fetishists, exhibitionists, people who are into body hair or eating shit—I'm not going to venture an opinion on what these are all about. As long as these people don't act out on their obsessions in ways that are hurtful to others, they are harmless enough. If there are hidden issues here, they are too obscure for me to delve into.

In general, obsessions and fascinations are probably attempts to get in touch with something that has been lost from the caller's life: attention, nurturing, being connected to one's body and emotions. While these fantasies may not be an effective way to deal with the problems, they are probably not harmful either. At worst, they mask the real problems and delay the necessity of working on them.

POWER GAMES

No matter what the scenario, almost all sexual fantasies are driven by the question: What will make me feel safe and in control? For many people, fantasy itself is enough—to be swept away into a world of excitement and stimulation where your every wish is fulfilled. For others, it feels safer to focus on something unusual or even bizarre, perhaps to make the experience more intense and absorbing. For still others, though, power over another person is what it takes to feel safe enough to step into the vulnerability of sexual activity.

Although the most obvious form of power games is the dominant / submissive scenario, many other types of calls also have power as the underlying theme.

The caller who wanted me to imitate several different animals, for example, was trying to overpower me by making me degrade myself. Not only did his demands require me to put out a lot of energy towards him, but he also tried to deny my humanity. I was to be a subhuman slave to his whims and to give him total power to control my behavior, to the point of denying my own reality.

This call demonstrates the emotional "power-over" dynamic that is more subtle than the physical power-over scenario of the typical "dominant" caller—the one who wants to exercise simple physical control over someone. The physical dominant sees only the most primitive level of power and is probably focused on physical violence as a way of self-protection in his life—not a very effective method in the long run.

While the direct and obvious degradation calls, such as those with animals, are at least a step "up" from the physical "brute-force" level of power, they are still at a low level of sophistication.

A more subtle version of the emotional power-over dynamic is found in the virgin seduction and child molestation calls, where the caller is the aggressor. Whether these fantasies are violent or gentle, the power dynamic is the same. The initiator of the action is not only controlling the events but is also "getting to" the person being seduced, turning them on. The perpetrator not only invades the victim's body and mind, he gets her to enjoy it too, making her an accomplice in her own victimization.

An excellent example of this kind of power play was the child molestation call I did as the teenage daughter who observed her father masturbating one night and confronted him about it in the morning. The girl started out innocent, curious and confused, progressed to becoming sexually involved, and ended by serving her father's needs, at the same time relishing the sexual power she had over him.

This complicity in victimization is a theme in the adult virgin seduction fantasy as well. Again, whether the seduction is brutal or gentle, the fantasy is that the virgin eventually succumbs. If the seduction is gentle, she is swept off her feet; if it is brutal, she acknowledges her need to be degraded. In either case, she surrenders her will as well as her body. She welcomes the invasion, becoming a slave to her seducer's needs and enjoying her defeat.

Both of these types of dominants attempt to gain control over another person through sex. Either they want to order someone around, or they want to invade the other person's self, shatter their boundaries and possess them. Such a strong need for control can only be based, I believe, on fear of being hurt oneself, either physically or emotionally or both. There is a desperation about this attitude that I find sad. I have more compassion for the dominant callers than for any other type.

The opposite side of the power dynamic, of course, is the submissive. Far from giving over their power, though, they are in fact the most controlling and manipulative of callers.

Looking at the virgin seduction and child molestation calls from the submissive viewpoint, for example, gives an entirely different picture of the same scenario. When the submissive is controlling the fantasy, the aggressor becomes a tool in the hands of the victim.

With one exception, all of the virgin seduction calls I have done where I was the aggressor were child molestation calls. I believe that these calls have all been attempts to re-enact incidents that happened in the callers' lives. The caller playing the part of the child is of course no longer a child. Rather he is an adult trying to gain mastery over a situation in which he was a victim.

Although the original situation was probably intensely stimulating both physically and emotionally, the aggressors were not setting out to meet the victim's needs. Instead, these people were dominants, acting under the power dynamics of dominants—trying to invade and control another person.

In order to maintain any sense of self, the victim of such an attack must find an effective strategy for fending off the invasion. Because the power imbalance is total, however, there is really no external method of defense. Physical and verbal resistance are both out of the question. The victim must therefore find an internal defense.

The strategy developed by the adult molested as a child is to fantasize a re-enactment of the incident, but with himself as the star attraction. Everything the aggressor does, he does to stimulate the victim, rather than to provide the aggressor with a feeling of power. If the aggressor orders the victim to undress, it is so that the victim can show off his body. If the victim's genitals are manipulated, it is to give him pleasure, rather than to give the aggressor the power of sexual arousal over him. If he is forced to perform oral sex on someone, it is to experience the power of sexual arousal over that person.

From the victim's point of view, then, everything is reversed. In the victim's mind, power, apparently the prerogative of the aggressor, is actually possessed by the victim. In this way, the victim regains control of the situation and hence recovers his sense of self. It is not that his boundaries have been shattered and his will destroyed. Rather, he is the center of attention, his needs are being met, and he has power over his perpetrators.

Callers who reinterpret the child molestation fantasy to become adult submissives carry this scenario to another level. They remove themselves from the specific abuse incident, generalizing and abstracting it.

Submissives are thus on a higher power trip than dominants. The submissive soaks up energy from his dominant, dictating every action and reveling in the stimulation it provides. Moreover, he gives all appearance of being innocent, allowing himself to be overpowered and engulfed. He is a manipulator *par excellence.*

And beyond even the heavy S/M submissive is a yet more subtle exercise of power: the high that someone can get from another person's responses to him. This, I think, is a supreme exercise of power—to see and feel and hear how intensely the other person is responding to the stimulation you give them. This, too, is one of the appeals of phone sex. Anyone can fantasize by themselves, but to have someone else responding to you intensifies the pleasure. I consider this a big part of my job, and I always do a lot of moaning, groaning and gasping, particularly with my higher-energy callers. I invariably get a good response to these carryings-on.

And, finally, there is the ultimate power trip—the flip side of the responsiveness game. While the partner who is <u>perceiving</u> the other person's responses experiences a sense of power, the partner <u>performing</u> the responses experiences even more power—the power of having given someone else the pleasure of your responses. As a performer I get some of this myself. Yet because my responses are acted, not real, my experience of power is not as intense as that of the callers who play this role.

I believe this is the most intense power high that sex has to offer. My sensuous callers, particularly the ones who do sensuous dominant calls, really get into it. When they submit to me, moaning, gasping, begging and exclaiming worshipfully over my body, they are getting high off the power of giving me power. These callers are really the ultimate submissives, and hence the ultimate power wielders.

It is clear that both the dominant and the submissive are driven by a need for power over others. The dominant seeks this power directly, the submissive indirectly. Yet both are limited by this need, dependent on other people to validate them. For how can you have power over others unless there are others present to have power over?

The submissive understands this dynamic and uses it to control the dominant. Yet the submissive, too, is caught in the same dilemma.

Although he is somewhat more self-sufficient than the dominant (since he can turn his own energy against himself), the submissive still needs the attention and devotion of the dominant. Left to himself with no dominant to manipulate, the submissive is like a co-dependent without an addict. He feels unworthy even of existence.

ATTENTION, AFFECTION AND VALIDATION

Overwhelming as the power issue is in sex, even deeper, I believe, is the need for attention, affection and validation. This need, in fact, is what ultimately drives not only the power issue but the escape and obsession issues as well.

As clearly as I could see the power dynamic going on in phone sex, I couldn't help but ask, "So what? What's the big deal about power, anyway?" It took me a long time to answer that question. It had been in my mind long before I started doing phone sex, and it haunted me more and more as I heard the power games, over and over, in my calls.

One obvious answer, of course, is that feelings of power cover up fears of helplessness and vulnerability. Yet this answer really just begs the question. What's so bad about helplessness and vulnerability, anyway?

Of course, many people have had scary experiences, as both children and adults, where they were hurt because they were powerless in some situation. Yet fear of being hurt did not seem to me to be a strong enough force to explain the intensity of the power struggles that I sometimes heard. Something more basic, more compelling, seemed to be at work here, particularly with the submissives.

So I started listening more critically to what was going on in the power calls—observing my own reactions as well as the callers'. And I began to notice more of my own feelings whenever I experienced power over someone or something in my life. What I concluded is that it's not really power, it's attention. A person who is wielding power is not just controlling people and situations; he's also getting lots of attention. Yet I still had to ask, "So what's the big deal with attention?"

Finally, a friend of mine put it together for me. We all come into the world helpless, dependent on other people to get our needs met. And only by getting attention from other people can we be sure that those needs are, indeed, going to be met. If no one notices us, if we are neglected, we will die. For this reason, newborn infants are programmed to crave attention.

It is, I believe, this desperate fear of oblivion, of being ignored and neglected, that drives the power issue so strongly. There are very few people in this world who have never felt threatened with neglect—at least emotional neglect, if not physical. This threat can be so frightening that it produces overwhelming feelings of neediness, inadequacy and vulnerability.

And sex, as I have said, is an area of life where strong feelings often get dumped. In sexuality, we are permitted to express ourselves, to be uninhibited. So if we are feeling insecure, we can use sex to obtain power and make ourselves feel safe. We can get attention and be sure that our needs are going to be met. We can become skilled performers, paragons of sensuality, and obtain recognition and validation and acquire a sense of accomplishment.

For all of these purposes, sexual <u>fantasy</u> is even more effective than physical sexual activity with other people. In fantasy, we can be in complete control of the situation. We can idealize the other participants and create the perfect setting, the perfect responses, the perfect activities. There are no limits to what we can do.

If we wonder what the appeal of pornography is, we need only look at the emotional deficits that most of us suffer from. Loneliness, fear of abandonment, lack of nurturing—sex promises to fix all of these things. Through its intensity we can escape our fears and inadequacies; by being the object of stimulation, we can get all the attention and validation we could possibly want; through its illusion of intimacy we can fulfill our need to be close to another human being.

Since the promises of real interactive sex are indeed false, it is only through fantasy that we can truly achieve these goals.

8

How It Has Affected Me

Early on in my phone sex work, before I started doing dominant calls, I got a call from a submissive who was a regular customer of the service but not one that I had worked with. Although the service knew that I did not do dominant calls, they gave me the call because he requested me. He had picked me "from the lineup"—the list of performers on call—because my name was new, and he evidently took it upon himself to train all new performers in how to do dominant calls.

I was not ready for this call. I didn't understand anything about submissives. I told him that I didn't do dominant calls, but he insisted that he was sure I would do okay. I went along with it because I knew that he was a regular customer and I felt that I should cater to him.

What he wanted was to be humiliated for having underdeveloped genitals. He said that he had a condition called "infantile genitalia" but that he was capable of erection and orgasm. He wanted to be taken to a party and humiliated—the standard submissive fantasies. I did an awkward job of it, using up the whole time limit. It was painful for me. I felt used and violated.

I was overwhelmed for days after this call. I was angry at the caller for manipulating me into something that I didn't feel comfortable with. I was angry at myself for giving in. I was angry at God for doing such a thing to someone.

Even in my volunteer crisis-line work, I hadn't had to deal with anything that triggered so much pain and anger in me. It took me weeks to work through it all. I talked to any of my friends who I thought could listen and be supportive, I prayed about it, I cried over it. I remained shaken for a long time, but I did eventually put the call behind me.

(I did talk to the supervisor at the phone service, who told me that I could have refused to do the call. They don't worry too much about pleasing regular customers. They have more business than they need anyway. I was too accustomed to being a service provider in my daytime job and thus felt the need to cater to a regular customer.)

Just a few months later, I got the exact same request from a different caller. I did the call without a hitch—smooth, professional, imaginative where I needed to be, a good actress, laughing convincingly, verbally abusing him. It only took me about five minutes. After I hung up, I sat back and asked myself, "What has happened to me?"

Working in any part of the sex business can make you jaded. What you're confronting is someone else's intimacy needs, but you're doing it from a place of detachment. Trying to deal with this paradox and integrate it into the rest of my life is a challenge.

Phone sex has opened up a new dimension of life for me. I will never see sex in quite the same way again. I have heard too much, participated in too much. I have different views of myself, of sexuality, of intimacy, of other people, than I had before I started in this business. And, although some of my phone sex work has been painful, I feel enriched by these experiences.

The most obvious effect of my phone sex work, of course, has been my education in sex. Although I was knowledgeable before I began, I was a lot more knowledgeable after a few weeks on the phones, and the more I learned, the more amazed I was at the limitlessness of the human imagination. When people are given the license that phone sex provides, it is amazing what they will come up with. My own fantasies seemed mild compared to some of what I heard on the phone.

I have redefined what is bizarre in sex, i.e., the boundaries of the normal are much farther out for me now. I think that there is, indeed, the potential for the bizarre in all of us. I would no longer be surprised if I found out that an executive at my daytime-job company had submissive fantasies in which he performed oral sex on a dog. Nor would I condemn him for it.

The more I listen to these fantasies on the phone, the more normal they seem, and the less I judge them. I see more clearly than ever how similar we all are and how much we hide from each other in "normal" life.

Having this kind of perspective has changed my outlook on life and people in general. Although I have long been aware that there is a lot more to people than what shows on the surface, these insights now constantly intrude on my everyday consciousness. I see the fragility of the facade, and I'm always looking for what I suspect lurks beneath it. When I see and hear a white Southern politician speaking on TV, projecting an image of friendliness, respectability and control, I think to myself, "I wonder if he has fantasies of being ass-fucked by a black man with a big dick?"

Sometimes it's hard for me to not be able to share these thoughts with the people around me. I have to keep reminding myself that a lot of them would be freaked out by these perceptions.

In fact, most people would be overwhelmed just by the graphic nature of my phone sex conversations. Sometimes wanting to be more explicit, I have to catch myself, when conversations about sex do come up (no pun intended) in normal conversation. Occasionally it's okay to be explicit, and it's nice to be able to be. At other times, I have to stop and remind myself that I'm not among my gay male friends or my sex-work colleagues.

Another side effect I've noticed is that sexual jokes aren't as funny as they used to be. A big part of the humor in sexual jokes, I think, is the disclosing of intense hidden feelings. I hear these feelings not only disclosed but expressed graphically all the time. These are the feelings that fuel the calls, that make things happen. Yes, they are intense.

I hear and participate in this intensity, and often I feel more sad than amused.

When I hear a joke about transvestitism, I may think back to the computer salesman I talked with last night, who wanted to put on women's panties and be humiliated in a shopping mall. Yet how could I share this memory and the sadness it evokes in me with the people who are laughing at the joke?

So in many ways I feel isolated. Since I work alone, at home, I don't have the opportunity to compare notes with other fantasy performers. In the last few years, though, I have developed friendships with other sex workers, mostly prostitutes, with whom I can share a lot of my experiences. And I also have some non-sex-worker friends I can talk with, although there is a limit to what they can listen to, understand and empathize with. The truth is, any kind of sex work is an isolating business, unless you're working in a house of prostitution.

There have been times, though, when I have used phone sex as my customers do, to ease my own loneliness, boredom, or feelings of in-adequacy (which everyone has from time to time). After all, I do get to talk to people, however briefly and superficially. And phone sex can be a way for me to feel competent and appreciated, if I'm not get-ting these needs met in other areas of my life.

I have also used phone sex, as I have mentioned, to work out my own anger and frustration at people in my life. For quite a while I used my dominant calls to express some of my anger at a man with whom I had had a difficult relationship. I simply pretended that he was the submissive caller and had a great time abusing and humiliating him. It was wonderful to have this outlet which helped me to get through my anger more quickly.

It has also been wonderful to be able to work in the sex business, which I was intrigued by long before I started working in it. This work has provided me with a unique, "inside" view of the world. One of my favorite books, is *Nell Kimball: Her Life as an American Madam* (Berkley Publishing Corporation, 1971). My original paperback copy is falling apart from having been over-read. I identified strongly with this intelligent insightful woman, who made a successful life for herself in what was at that time (late nineteenth and early twentieth century) strictly a man's world.

Phone sex, though, is a better job than prostitution. Not only is it safer, but it also provides me with the essence of the experience that I was looking for: to really get into someone else's head, into their fantasies. That's where the real inside story is.

One reason I've been able to gain access to these fantasies is that as a performer I am not threatening to my callers. I'm often amused when demanding callers try to harass or degrade me. "If they only knew..." I think—i.e., that I'm an intelligent, articulate, well-educated professional woman rather than the marginally literate working-class woman that they probably perceive me as. If they did know, they would probably be intimidated. Not knowing, they feel safe and reveal their needs and vulnerability, whether they realize they are doing that or not.

As a fantasy performer I can often connect with people whom I normally would probably never meet. One night, for example, I was doing one of my rare local calls, and I ended with one of my standard lines, "I guess you'll be able to get to sleep now." "Well, no, actually," he replied, "I'm going to work now." (It was about 1 a.m. local time.) He was in the military, and his job at that time was to be a third-shift guard at the gate of a nearby military base, where demonstrators were keeping up protest lines 24 hours a day. We talked a little about what that was like for him—the combination of tension, fear, and boredom. I didn't bother to tell him that I had a number of friends out there on the protest lines and in fact had been out there myself on occasion.

As a confirmed pacifist, I don't often get the opportunity to be intimate with military people. Yet after this call I felt a closeness with and compassion for this man, and I got a different view of a situation that I thought I already knew all about.

Moments of intimacy like this sometimes make me feel that phone sex is my real life and that my "other" life is the sham, the deception. This feeling is intensified by the contrast between my phone sex work and my daytime job in data processing. I could hardly have picked a second job that was more different from my primary one.

Sometimes it's hard for me to believe that phone sex is indeed a job, that I get paid for it. I'm used to working with machines—abstract, logical machines. Computers define their own reality, and it's a highly structured, limited and controlled reality. Phone sex customers define their own reality, too, of course, but it's a loosely structured, unlimited reality. Although there is a certain pattern to the process of sexual arousal and release, there are many diverse and meandering paths to the goal.

My data processing job is to put boundaries around problems and help people to gain control of information. My job as a fantasy performer, on the other hand, is to get people off—in effect, to remove boundaries and make them lose control, in a physical as well as an emotional way. It's like being a comedian except that the emotion I work with is lust instead of amusement. I really am, indeed, a performer.

And being "on stage" has given me a detachment and self-confidence that I didn't have before. Although I don't get performance reviews for my phone sex work, I do get feedback from my customers, and the overwhelming majority of this feedback is positive—I do a good job and I know it. Those times when I am not successful at getting someone off, I can see clearly that it's their problem, not mine. If they can't get off on my stimulation, it's either because they are demanding callers who are simply burned out on sex or unable to let themselves go, or they are those rare people for whom phone sex just doesn't do it.

I've carried this perspective over into other areas of my life, too. If I'm having difficulty dealing with someone, I am more inclined to assign responsibility to them now instead of taking it all on myself as I used to. I know I'm capable of dealing difficult people, and I also know that some people are more of a challenge than I really need. I can let those people go now with no feeling of failure. They have needs that I can't meet, that's all, just like some of my callers.

Some of my best lessons have been from dominant or demanding callers. I see so clearly now their fears of inadequacy and vulnerability that I am no longer intimidated by this personality type. Now when I have to deal with a domineering person in a business meeting, I often see them as similar to my demanding callers. Remembering the desperation and neediness I have heard in those voices, I feel a mixture of compassion, contempt and amusement towards these people. This image helps me to listen beyond the words, the gestures, the behaviors. Now I see someone who feels threatened, not someone who is threatening to others.

In fact, I now see the corporate world as a whole being driven by needs and desires quite different from the apparent striving for money, information and power. And this insight sometimes makes me wonder which is more real—my daytime activities or my night-time ones. Perceiving the undercurrents of fear, insecurity and loneliness in the business world makes the world of phone sex fantasy seem more genuine and authentic by comparison. In phone sex, people at least admit to having feelings!

Despite the occasional heaviness of my phone sex work, though, often the perceptions I bring back from it are more amusing than philosophical. One day, for example, during a work break at my daytime job, I stopped to look at some space that was being remodeled into executive offices. They were almost complete but no one had been moved into them yet. As I looked around at the plush carpets, polished redwood cabinets, and private views of the outside landscape, I thought to myself, "What a great place for a sexual fantasy!"

I've also developed an amusing image of one of the people I work with— a highly competent, strong-willed woman in one of our financial departments. She keeps a tight rein on the operations of that department, zealously guarding her position and her extensive knowledge, unwilling to share much responsibility with anyone. She is also suspicious of computers and often difficult for us in the systems department to deal with. Whenever her name comes up in conversation, I am tempted to say, "She dresses in black leather and always carries a whip."

Humor, of course, is partly a way of dealing with a heaviness that could overwhelm me if I let it. I do feel sad. I grieve for the losses that I know some of my callers have suffered. Although I don't know all the specifics, I do know that they have lost touch with some part of themselves that they expect sexual fantasy to restore.

Yet for all the sadness and intensity, this work does not in fact overwhelm me. I feel instead a real sense of accomplishment. I started out scared, not sure that I could really do this work. Yet I learned to do it, through failures as well as successes, and I've learned about people in a way that I never could have otherwise. Not only hearing about but actually participating in their fantasies, I see how much these people are like myself. How simple and universal are our needs, despite the complexity and variety of our behaviors!

And so out of what might appear at first glance to be exploitative experiences, I have developed more acceptance and compassion—for myself as well as for others. I see more clearly and immediately now how vulnerable and yet how strong and creative we all are. I feel closer to people than I ever did before.

Although I have felt great sadness about some calls, I also feel hopeful when I see how positive are the needs that drive the fantasies. I believe deeply in the goodness of life and of people. I feel blessed to have been given the talents and opportunities I have to do phone sex work. I am privileged to have traveled these paths of pain and darkness and to have found hope and joy as well.

9

Who Are These People, Anyway?

At a nightclub in the city, the phone sex company is holding its annual Christmas party. The air is thick with smoke, especially at the bar. (I have never seen so many smokers as among this group.) Women dressed in flamboyantly suggestive outfits mingle with their more plainly dressed, slightly embarrassed male escorts. In the only room that has sufficient lighting, a young woman in black fishnet hose and gold lame minidress jumps up onto the buffet and poses for a photograph, ass and bust thrust out, skirt riding up her thighs, while the less flamboyant secretary, wearing jeans and dark shirt, sits between her open legs, grinning. They both laugh raucously as the manager snaps their picture.

On the dance floor, where the DJ is playing records too loud for anyone to speak over, a few couples dance half-heartedly. Another performer saunters out to the middle of the floor and starts dancing wildly and sensuously. A male performer dressed in tight black pants and high-heeled boots, shirt half unbuttoned, joins her, and they try to outdo each other with outrageous moves.

Back at the bar, a small group of women sit trading tips on calls, customers and phone sex companies:

"Tamara's is the best to work for. They treat you like shit, but they give you lots of calls."
"I give my customers three minutes. That's it. Then I tell them they're out of time."
"Don't they ever object?"
"Fuck, no. They're lying there with their dick in their hand, they're not lookin' at the clock."

"I have about five or six standard scenes I go through. I keep track of who I've given what to, so I don't repeat the same scene."

"I run through my standard line, and I always end up by saying, 'And you just came in my mouth, didn't you?' They always say yes."

"I put my submissive callers in a clothes dryer and bounce them around."

"I stick a hot curling iron up their ass. They love it."

One of the women takes a lipstick out of her purse and applies it deftly to her arching lips. "This is 'Clitoral Pink'," she explains.

A male performer, dressed in drag—black minidress, hose and spike heels—joins the group. He does calls with both gay and straight men, imitating a female voice for the straight-male callers.

"When they ask me if they can play with my tits, I tell them, 'Only if you'll hum "Jingle Bells" for me first'. I tell them that the one who does the best job will get a free call after January 1st."

While many of the people at the party fit the stereotype of those who work in the sex business—cynical, callous, flaunting their sexuality—others are quieter and more ordinary. Several are middle-aged housewives, either married or divorced, some with children. One has been in the business for over six years, having given up a career as an accountant. She defends her choice of occupation staunchly:

"It's a better job than the one I left. I can be home when my son gets home from school. I don't have to commute, buy clothes for work, or put up with someone else's rules and schedules. Back when I started, before the competition got so intense, I was making $1,000 a week. Now it's less, but I bought my house with the proceeds of those early years."

These arguments are echoed by many of the women performers. Phone sex is better paying and has a better working environment than most of the available unskilled or semi-skilled jobs.

Some performers try to collect as many regular customers as they can, and they keep files on each one's preferences. Since we get paid extra for "request" calls, where a customer asks for a particular performer, this is probably the way to make the most money with the fewest number of calls. Other performers, though, myself included, prefer not to bother with building up a regular clientele. As one of them put it, "Once is enough, talking to these guys."

Performers are insistent that they are actresses or actors, not prostitutes. They see their job as respectable, if not socially accepted. If they lack respect, it is more for their customers than for themselves. They acknowledge, however, that this viewpoint is not generally accepted. Many performers do not tell family and friends what they do for a living. The ex-accountant explains:

"I work while my son is in school and then again at night after he goes to bed. He doesn't know what I do for a living; he thinks I do some sort of accounting work over the phone. I'll tell him when he gets older, or if he starts asking questions. But he doesn't need to know now. I have a sound-proof room in the house, with a separate phone line that I simply unplug when I'm not working."

In other cases, however, the work intrudes on family life unavoidably. Another performer lived for more than a year in a one-room apartment with her partner. "You can imagine what this was like, being in the business I'm in," she said. "I work most of the night, while he has a daytime job and has to sleep. It was such a relief when we could finally afford to move into a larger apartment."

The problem here was more the noise than the subject matter. Male partners of female performers take the job in stride, understanding that phone sex is fantasy, not prostitution, and that it has little if anything to do with their relationships. Most of them share in their partners' cynicism and are amused by the customer-bashing that pervades company get-togethers.

"God, I hate Saturday nights! The worst perverts call on Saturday
nights!" (I haven't found this to be true, myself.)
"Do you know how many horses I've sucked off?"
"Have you talked to that guy in Toronto who always has to come
three times? I hate doing calls with him."
"I'm glad I don't have to do all of these weird things just to get off.
At least I'm normal."

This judgmentalism even comes through during working hours,
from both performers and call order clerks. Typical remarks I have
gotten from clerks, when giving me orders, are: "This guy's out in
Podunk, with all the other winners of the world." Or: "This guy
wants penis torture. Sounds like fun, huh?"

Even other performers occasionally get jabbed. One night, for example, an order clerk told me about a new performer that had just
started. She told the woman that she would withhold the more bizarre calls at first, but the newcomer replied, "Oh, that's okay, you
can give me anything. I'm a psych major." All of us regulars had a
good laugh over that one. We pride ourselves on being hardened
and worldly wise. Our kind of knowledge is not book learning.

Judgmentalism extends even to the owners and managers. "The
management attitude here," one performer told me, "seems to be
that the girls are sleazy and the callers are perverts." Yet this attitude should be no surprise. Phone sex is not a business that normally attracts people interested in performing a social service.

Yet many performers do feel that they may be helping to contain
acts of sexual aggression. "Better that some guy should fantasize
with me about raping a 4-year-old than go out and do it. I hope he
gets it out of his system this way."

We hope, yes, but we don't know. I suspect, myself, that fantasy
provides only temporary relief, and that in the long run it aggra-
vates the problem. Putting all of that energy and attention into the
fantasy strengthens it. But none of us really knows. We can ask
people who are arrested for sex crimes whether they use pornogra-

phy, but we can't find out whether the majority of people who use pornography refrain from acting out. My anecdotal evidence indicates that they do refrain, but that evidence is not only unreliable, it is also limited.

Whatever effect the sex business has on the customer, however, it does provide work for a large group of unskilled people. And it is always available. Until our society becomes emotionally healthy (and I'm not holding my breath on that one, although I have some hope), the sex business will always be with us. And it doesn't take much initiative or talent to get into it. There's a chronic shortage of workers. If you want to work in the sex business, just show up and apply, or find a street corner and start soliciting customers.

Although some high-priced escorts do take a professional pride in their work and are highly skilled at entertaining their clients, both sexually and socially, most sex work does not attract upwardly mobile people, or people who expect a lot of attention and acknowledgment from their jobs. (As one friend of mine commented, these are not people who are concerned about their resumes.) It does not feature regular performance reviews or provide opportunities for advancement. With the possible exceptions of acting and writing, most of the jobs in the sex business do not constitute a profession or a career.

Many of the jobs, in fact, are low-paying, or have poor working conditions, or both. Erotic dancers, for example, have to pay the nightclub to work there, and it is not uncommon for film or video workers to be sexually harassed or exploited by their employers. Phone sex, by contrast, is one of the better jobs in the sex industry. It pays reasonably well, has a good working environment, and provides personal freedom and room for creativity that are rare in any job.

And all this in a job that requires no formal education (there are no college degrees in sex work). Phone sex does demand somewhat more acting ability than many other types of sex work. Because it is pure fantasy, the roles you may have to play are unlimited in scope and variety. Even prostitution and acting in films or videos have some limits imposed by physical reality.

Phone sex is a relative newcomer on the the sex business scene. It started in the late 1970s. The company I worked for was one of the oldest and most reputable. They treated their employees fairly and tried to provide quality service for their customers. (A number of regular customers have told me that performers in my company do the best job of any they have tried out.) Performers were provided with insurance and vacation benefits, just as in any other job. Those who derive their major source of income from phone sex were given the most calls; those of us who worked part-time took the overflow.

Having performers work out of their homes is, of course, a savings on office space but also provides a better atmosphere for the work. There are some phone sex companies that do provide office space and telephones for the performers, but these are not private offices; they are large, open areas. Trying to do a good job under these conditions is a lost cause. These calls may be okay for customers who just need to hear a little dirty talk, but for those who want a real fantasy, they're a disaster. Uninhibited though performers are, those who really get into role-playing can do a much better job in privacy. My company would never think of asking a performer to do a call with an audience listening in.

With the number of phone sex services proliferating, some of them try to play a certain "angle" to be unique. They may, for example, advertise anal sex or she-males. Or they may, on the other hand, try to downplay the sleazy aspect, appeal to a "higher class" of people: one of my company's ads simply shows a picture of a telephone, with the words "SEX SYMBOL" underneath. There is at least one service that advertises they have a hundred different performers, of all ethnic and racial groups. (No doubt what they have is about a dozen good actresses who can play these different roles. The regular customer who told me about this service was disappointed when I told him the truth.)

Live phone sex, of course, is not the only type available. There are varying degrees of live versus recorded phone sex, of various costs and qualities. There are also "dating service" lines, usually "900" numbers, where people can connect up with someone else who is looking for a partner. And for all types of phone sex, there are gay as well as straight lines. The gay lines are predominantly male, however, except for some "900" numbers for lesbians. Pure fantasy lines for lesbians are rare.

The recordings are the cheapest type of phone sex. These usually run for several minutes and consist of one person (or sometimes two or three people) reading through a script. This is usually a simple story fantasy, but it can be just a few minutes of "hot talk". Some lines give the customer a choice of types of scenarios—"front," "back," "two-girl," "kinky," "dominant."

Some lines are a combination of live and recorded. On one type of line, the customer can call in and talk live to a performer, but then other customers can call and listen in on this conversation—both sides of it. Voyeurism on the phone...

Other lines are pseudo-live: they are recordings, but are interspersed with long pauses, during which the customer is supposed to put in his two cents worth. The next offering from the performer is then supposed to be a response to the customer's input.

With all types of lines, the quality varies tremendously. This is true of the technical aspects such as the telephone connection and recording as well as the skill of the performer. Generally, a customer will get the best service from talking to a live performer, even though many of these services are mediocre. Really good performers who take pride in their work are few and far between. As with any other job, many of the workers do not really like the work. "Some of these places," one regular customer told me, "all you get is a lot of heavy breathing and 'Fuck me! Fuck me!'"

Similar to many other lines of work is how differently the workers and customers perceive the work, each other, and themselves. To the workers, the sex business is a job, no more exciting than any other job. To the owners and managers, it's a business. Both of these groups feel superior to the customers. (If this attitude seems calloused, consider that it's difficult to have much respect for someone when the only contact you have with him is when you're exploiting his neediness. You might have compassion for him but not respect.) Yet to the customers, the sex business is exciting and stimulating, and they see themselves as being in control, being catered to.

These differences in attitude, I suppose, are the same as in any class structure. Servants, knowing all the "dirt" on their employers, often have a rather low opinion of them. Yet the upper class people who employ them often perceive these people as something less than themselves, as staff whose opinions don't matter anyway. Or perhaps they don't even think that the servants have opinions. Likewise, many men who patronize the sex business seem to believe that the workers either enjoy catering to the customers' needs or that they don't have any opinions about them, and certainly not negative opinions!

A few customers, though, are curious about the sex business workers and wonder what they think about themselves and their work. I occasionally get callers who want to interview me, to find out what I'm like in real life. (I even got a college student once who said he was writing a paper on phone sex.) I never tell them the whole truth, especially my opinions about the work and the customers; they'd be insulted, I fear.

Some customers are actually perceptive enough to figure out that many sex workers are egotistical exhibitionists who delight in all the attention they get. Yet never have I known a customer to take this observation far enough to figure out how exploited he himself is, at least in monetary terms. It amazes me, the amount of money that many straight men will pay for sexual stimulation, even without release. In fact, one of my gay friends has often remarked that the most outstanding characteristic of straight sexual relationships, as he observes them, is the frequency with which money is involved in the transaction, whether it's pornography, prostitution, dating, or marriage. This situation reflects the still patriarchal structure of our society, where men have the economic power, women the emotional power.

Even aside from the money, the sex business does seem to me to use up an inordinate amount of time, energy and money that could be put to more fulfilling and constructive use. I suppose this is another advantage to phone sex, compared to other types of the sex business: you don't have to drive anywhere or expose yourself to any physical risk (including, for some, the risk of being seen). You just pick up the phone in the privacy of your home and spend only as long as you need to, getting your needs met.

Phone sex is one of the cheaper types of the sex business businesses to start and maintain. The biggest expenses are advertising, telephones and credit validating services. Phone sex has some similarities to radio, which is the cheapest journalistic medium. Neither requires a lot of office space, professional photography, printing presses, or spacious studios or other work areas. The effect depends on the imagination, which takes up no physical space.

Phone sex is unique in the sex industry. Like written stories, it is pure fantasy, yet unlike written stories, it is the customer's fantasy, not the writer's. And, unlike most other forms of pornography (photographs, films and videos, erotic dancing, stories), the object of phone sex is for the customer to reach orgasm through direct interaction with the performer. The only other form of the sex business that provides this amount of direct interaction is the "peep booths" where the customer usually masturbates while viewing, and perhaps talking with, a performer through a window.

Phone sex, then, provides a level of customer control and direct interaction with another person that is not available in any other type of the sex business. It is a lot like prostitution, only without the physical limitations and risks.

Regardless of the level of customer involvement or satisfaction, working in the sex business inevitably provides a view of life and people very different from that of the "mainstream" culture. Those of us who work in the sex business are a largely unacknowledged underground, outcasts to some degree. This position gives us sometimes a feeling of privilege but other times feelings of resentment and disappointment because we are not appreciated or recognized. Only when we get together can we share among ourselves our difficulties, give each other advice, or get some acknowledgment for our own achievements.

It is an achievement to have worked in the sex business. It's a type of work that most people are simply not able to do—even phone sex, which doesn't have many physical prerequisites. In spite of the supposedly open attitude our culture has, many people are uncomfortable with sexuality, or maybe they can't act, or can't talk about sex, or they just don't work well in isolation. Many more people can do the work for a while but get burned out: one to two years is usually the limit on phone sex work, although many drop out after a few weeks or months. Those who stay are able to develop a detachment that allows them to separate themselves from the roles they play.

Although the sex business is rarely if ever a fulfilling career, how many jobs really are? Compared to my other career its greatest drawback, from my viewpoint, is its lack of variety. But, again, how many jobs provide variety? Among the unskilled and semi-skilled occupations, not many, and after a number of years even the supposedly glamorous professions such as data processing get old. Against this backdrop, the sex business is not a bad way to put in a few years.

I still feel that if anyone is exploited by the sex business, it is the customers, and perhaps our society as a whole. The customers are the ones who pay, in time and energy as well as in money, and there are many pressing social needs that could be met with some of that energy and money. Yet I see the existence of the sex business as a symptom of the things that are wrong with our culture, not a cause.

Given the complexity of the causes, I don't expect this symptom to go away anytime soon.

Phone sex and other types of sex business are here to stay for a good while. Non-intimate sex is usually the last addiction that people deal with, even after they give up drinking, smoking, drugs, gambling, over-eating or over-working. For not only does it provide a temporary escape from pain, it also provides an illusion of intimacy, which is a real need.

To some extent, the sex business serves a similar function for the workers as for the customers. It's a living for many, yes, but it can also provide an illusion of power, or at least of superiority. Hence it can be an outlet for anger against the customers and against society. Yet sex work can also be enlightening, as it allows us to see people trying to meet their emotional as well as their physical needs, and to see people in their neediness and vulnerability is to see the hope as well as the despair.